Selling Something Nobody Needs

**False Doctrine Cleaned Me Up!
But God Saved Me!**

Robert Anderson

Detroit, MI USA

Selling Something Nobody Needs: False Doctrine Cleaned Me Up! But God Saved Me!

Copyright © 2017 Robert L. Anderson

All scripture quotations, unless otherwise indicated, are taken from the HOLY BIBLE, KING JAMES VERSION and are marked (KJV).

Scripture quotations marked (ESV) are from the ESV® Bible (The Holy Bible, English Standard Version®), copyright © 2001 by Crossway, a publishing ministry of Good News Publishers. Used by permission. All rights reserved.

All rights reserved. No part of this publication may be reproduced, stored in a retrieval system, or transmitted in any form or by any means – electronic, mechanical, photocopy, recording, or any other – except for brief quotations in printed reviews, without the prior permission of the publisher.

NOTE:

Bullet points and bold text are added by the author to provide emphasis on the borrowed references.

Truth Seekers Read Publications
P. O. Box 23345 • Detroit, MI 48223
E-mail: truthseekersread@att.net
URL: http://www.truthseekersread.com

ISBN 13:   978-0-9987221-0-8
ISBN 10:   0-9987221-0-3

Editing by Patricia Hicks and Jerome Smith

Cover, and Interior design by Robert L. Anderson

Printed in the United States of America

TABLE OF CONTENTS

Introduction 1

Chapter One
God Can Save Anybody 3

Chapter Two
Losing People, Places, and Hope 11

Chapter Three
Trust God (Depending on Mother Rose) 17

Chapter Four
Don't Depend On Self (Proverbs 3:5) 33

Chapter Five
Broken Connections 39

Chapter Six
It's Not about Me 43

Chapter Seven
Question Everybody 53

Chapter Eight
God Knows - Story of the Nails 71

Chapter Nine
Believe God is Able ~ Healing 75

Chapter Ten
The Doctrine Of Israel In Retrospect 79

Chapter Eleven
The Art of Twisting Scriptures 87

Chapter Twelve
Israel Spiritual School of Theology (I.S.S. of T.) 133

Chapter Thirteen
Other Groups: Hebrew ~ Israel ~ Jews 169

Glossary 199

Resources Web Internet Links Verified Live: 201

About the Author 205

Selling Something Nobody Needs tells how God's grace, mercy, and protection preserved Robert Anderson from very dangerous surroundings in Detroit's inner city from youth to mature adulthood. God used some very remarkable circumstances to ultimately bring Pastor Anderson to genuine faith in Christ.

Unknown previously to Pastor Anderson, I believe his true story is a remarkable answer to the prayer requests of several students in my Bible Discussion Club where I taught at Detroit's Cass Technical High School, students who closed out their senior year with an unforgettable prayer meeting held at their request.

One prayer request I will never forget was that God would make it possible for the black pastors in Detroit to have access to the kind of Bible teaching I had shared with these students. Pastor Anderson, and his pastor, Pastor Emery Moss, Jr. of Strictly Biblical Bible Teaching Ministries, represent how God has worked to continue to answer these student prayers. Read Pastor Anderson's remarkable life story, and how God used even the mistaken ministry of a little-known false cult to accomplish His purpose. Don't miss this thrilling, uplifting account!

Jerome Smith, author of The New Treasury of Scripture Knowledge and The Ultimate Cross Reference Treasury.

INTRODUCTION

I wrote this book to provide an inside view of what can happen when people join churches, and they don't know enough to ask for the church's Doctrinal Statement and how to prove all things and hold fast that which is good according to 1 Thessalonians 5:21. Why would we expect a person coming to Jesus Christ, perhaps for the first time in their life, to know more than the Ethiopian Eunuch Acts 8:30-38 about Jesus, God, or the Scriptures, who admitted that he did not understand what he was reading, and that he needed a teacher? And yet we, the church, often mock people for joining false doctrinal Churches and cults that give the illusion of being Christian.

I am aware that there we will be those that read what I now label as "un-believable teachings" sprinkled around Scriptures used out of context, and they will say I could never have believed or practice those things. I'll simply thank God that you did not have to experience what I expose in this book. It appears that many think the Great Commission (Matthew 28:19) is about those that have never heard about Jesus, but what about those that were snared by agents of Satan passing themselves off as angels of light 2 Corinthians 11:13-15?

Some Christian brothers and sisters may think the book's target audience is black people (Afro-Americans), but this is not true. All people need to know what these groups teach as it is related to you, and how to witness and teach biblically against these errors. Error has no color boundaries, and neither does truth.

It is my hope that the experiences I shared in this book might be a deterrent for those heading down the same path whether the individual is within or outside of the Church. And to all others, I pray they understand the importance of being ready to give a sound Biblical answer to every man 1 Peter 3:15.

James 5:20 "Let him know, that he which converteth the sinner from the error of his way shall save a soul from death, and shall hide a multitude of sins."

Pastor Robert Anderson
To God Be the Glory!

~*~

A special thanks to my beautiful wife Jo Ann Anderson, for her continued love, patience, and support for over 30 years.

This book is dedicated to my late mother,
Vivian Barnes.

CHAPTER ONE
GOD CAN SAVE ANYBODY

God doesn't save devils, but He saved a wretch like me. I had finally hit rock bottom. I was homeless, a bum, and a drug addict. There were sores and abscesses all over my body from shooting up, and I had used up and collapsed all my veins. I remember the times I was badly in need of a fix, but I had no veins. In agony and disgust, searching for a vein to shoot up, I would throw the syringe across the room with one hand only to go pick it up with the other hand. I felt torn inside of myself ~ wanting the drug and not wanting it, as if there was a battle going on within me. I was tired of being an addict, but I didn't want to be sick, dreading the withdrawal of heroin only to do it all over again. This was a madness that I could not escape. How many times had I cried and tried to go free only to run back to my captor again? I could not stand to look at my own body, I pained at what I had become, and I saw no hope.

HOPELESS IN THE DOPE HOUSE:

I was in a dope house one day, around 1977, and a friend of mine told me about a church he had been attending, The Spiritual Israel Church & Its Army. He asked me to attend and reluctantly I did. Even though I felt so embarrassed and so low. The few clothes I had were dirty and worn, and I didn't even own a change of underwear (with holes in them). I cleaned up the best that I could, and he loaned me a tie. I remember choosing to sit in the back of the church. I felt so lost, hurt, and unloved. But the lady minister was preaching that God loves you and that you are somebody. It was as if she was preaching directly to me. I couldn't get that out of my head, and I still don't remember anything else she said. I thought about my condition. God Loves ME, I asked myself? I thought about the sores over my body. I am somebody? I needed to hear more.

I wish I could say I stopped using heroin that very day, but I didn't. I continued in my old way of life, thinking that when "I" *get myself* together, I will go back to that church. But what I didn't know at that time is that Satan hears you, and he will do all he can to keep you from getting yourself together. You can't do it without God. In my life, the Bible was a closed book, and you can't flee something you are chasing after.

"Submit yourselves therefore to God. Resist the devil, and he will flee from you (**James 4:7**).

I was now outdoors, homeless, pitiful, feeling sorry for myself, blaming others, and an unwelcome sight. My sister opened her door to me and allowed me to sleep across the bed with the children (Who peed in the bed…but what could I say? It was their bed). I remember feeling so helpless, hopeless, and crying out for help. I wanted to get away and thought I was going to lose my mind. I felt as if no one could hear or see me. But the words I had heard when I had attended that service at The Spiritual Israel Church & Its Army still rang in my ears and gave me comfort. Nathaniel no longer had to take me to church; I didn't have a car, but I would ride my bicycle to church. I gave my hand joining the church in 1978. Yes, I came as I was - with habits, addiction, and all. I wanted to be in the service, I wanted God's help. The church had weekly services as well, and I would slip away from my street life and attend.

HOPELESS TO HOPE:

I got a job over on Clay Street off the Chrysler Freeway at an industrial plant that made rubber parts for the automotive industry. I worked afternoons. The job didn't pay much, but thank God I was working. In the winter time after midnight, boy did it get cold waiting on the Clairmont bus hugging the buildings while trying to stay warm. I endured the wind that would whip up off the Chrysler Freeway, and I stayed with that job until I found another job as a security guard. I rented an apartment on Gladstone near 12th street. I didn't have any furniture, but it was mine (no more pissy baby bed for me). I was so thankful. I found a couple of kitchen chairs out on the curb, scrubbed them down, and set them up together to sleep on near the radiator. Not long afterwards, I found an old dresser with the drawers and a bed that someone had thrown out. I paid a guy who owned a truck to help me haul them back to my apartment. I washed them down with Pine-Sol with a smile on my face, all the while thanking God. I can't remember where I found the old couch, but I got that too. I saw some empty milk crates, brought them back to my apartment, washed them down, covered them, and set them up as end-tables and a coffee table. I bought some cheap plastic curtains and put them up to the windows. It was clean, and it was home. Even though it was not like what I once had in my life, the difference now was God.

> **Philippians 4:12** "I know both how to be abased, and I know how to abound: every where and in all things, I am instructed both to be full and to be hungry, both to abound and to suffer need."

My only problem as a security guard was that I didn't want to bust (arrest) anyone for stealing in the store. Not that I was going to allow anyone to steal, but I had mixed emotions because of my past with the law. I thought I could be a cool brother (with a badge) and just warn them to put the items back. But I soon learned that some people are just looney. I did have a gun that had to be checked in and out on the premises.

Often people ask me what, when, and how I got off drugs. I replied, "I can't tell you the day nor the hour. All I know is I kept attending services, hearing the Word of God, learning to depend on and trust in God. It was like I opened my eyes one day realizing that drugs were on one-side of the street and I was on the other." God was separating me from my previous life. Of course, there were struggles, things, and people I wanted to cling to, but God helped me and caused me to realize that I didn't live there anymore. In other words, I was the onion, and God was the One who peeled me. He began to replace the friends I thought I was giving up with people who feared God (not that they or I were perfect). I learned that there is no loss in God.

> **Proverbs 3: 5** "Trust in the LORD with all thine heart; and lean not unto thine own understanding. 6 In all thy ways acknowledge him, and he shall direct thy paths."

QUIT SHOOTING-DOPE, SMOKING AND EATING MEAT:

By 1979, I was a regular tithe paying member in The Spiritual Israel Church & Its Army. The God of Israel had cleaned me up, I was no longer shooting drugs, and I had stopped smoking cigarettes (but not marijuana). I even stopped eating meat for the wrong reason. Not that the church taught this, but it was due to erroneous teachings from various other sources that I had read or heard, such as the Nation of Islam. They would reference Scriptures on the dietary laws such as Leviticus chapter eleven where Moses and Aaron spoke to the children of Israel about what beasts of the earth and in the waters that we are not supposed to eat:

> Leviticus 11:4-8, 10-12 Nevertheless these shall ye not eat of them that chew the cud, or of them that divide the hoof: as the camel, because he cheweth the cud, but divideth not the hoof; he is unclean unto you. And the coney, because he cheweth the cud, but divideth not the hoof; he is unclean unto you. And the hare, because he

cheweth the cud, but divideth not the hoof; he is unclean unto you. And the swine, though he divide the hoof, and be clovenfooted, yet he cheweth not the cud; he is unclean to you. Of their flesh shall ye not eat, and their carcase shall ye not touch; they are unclean to you.

And all that have not fins and scales in the seas, and in the rivers, of all that move in the waters, and of any living thing which is in the waters, they shall be an abomination unto you: They shall be even an abomination unto you; ye shall not eat of their flesh, but ye shall have their carcases in abomination. Whatsoever hath no fins nor scales in the waters, that shall be an abomination unto you.

The good thing about not eating meat is that I learned discipline and that I could refrain from things that I craved, not realizing that God would use this discipline in other areas of my life. However, I was not aware that Christians are not under the Mosaic Law, but the Law of Christ, and Gentiles (non-Israelites) were never under the Mosaic Law. Although in The Spiritual Israel Church & Its Army we were taught that we were not Christians or Gentiles but the real Israelites. I was not aware of the Scripture where God spoke to Peter about what was clean in Acts the eleventh chapter:

Acts 11:5-10 "I was in the city of Joppa praying: and in a trance I saw a vision, A certain vessel descend, as it had been a great sheet, let down from heaven by four corners; and it came even to me: Upon the which when I had fastened mine eyes, I considered, and saw fourfooted beasts of the earth, and wild beasts, and creeping things, and fowls of the air. And I heard a voice saying unto me, Arise, Peter; slay and eat. But I said, Not so, Lord: for nothing common or unclean hath at any time entered into my mouth. But the voice answered me again from heaven, What God hath cleansed, that call not thou common. And this was done three times: and all were drawn up again into heaven."

Today I still don't eat beef or pork, but it is now a matter of choice rather than an erroneous interpretation of Scripture. When asked about not eating meat, I never failed to point out that if there is a famine in the land, don't be surprised if you see me outside roasting a pig. I'm not a fool, and I will eat what God provides.

I remember once when I was late for church because I was staring in the closet at all the ties I had accumulated and could not make up my mind which tie to wear. For some reason that day It was a real task. Then the Holy Spirit said to me, "When you first came to the church you didn't own a tie or anything else. You had to borrow a tie. Now you are being late for My service because you can't figure out which one to wear?" I just grabbed the first tie my hand touched and left for service. I am reminded of the Scripture:

> Joel 2:13 "And rend your heart, and not your garments, and turn unto the LORD your God: for he is gracious and merciful, slow to anger, and of great kindness, and repenteth him of the evil."

STRUGGLING AND ADMITTING THE TRUTH TO MYSELF:

Yet I was still hustling pills and marijuana. I was good at it and was making a lot of money. I wanted to do something different, but I didn't know how. As foolish as it may sound, **I counted it as being blessed**. No one told me any different, and I paid my tithes and was on the deacon board. I did everything that was asked of me (and then some) in the church. I was a zealous Israelite (we didn't call ourselves Christians).

Around 1982, smoking cocaine was beginning to be more popular. On one occasion, I remember leaving church on a Sunday and going looking up some acquaintances to indulge in this activity. They didn't come looking for me; I went looking for them on a Sunday afternoon after attending church. Long story short, I had a bad experience trying to smoke it with cologne, and I called EMS because I couldn't breathe and thought I was dying. Alone, lying on a cot in the emergency room, it was as if the Holy Spirit was talking to me like a father to a son: "I have gotten you off of dope, and this and that, and I have washed you, healed your body of the sores, etc. and cleaned you up. Why on earth would you want to go backwards and pick something else up?" The voice was soft, it did not whip me, but it convicted me. That was the end of my cocaine experience. Even so, "I still had so much to learn...."

All drugs were now a thing of the past. But I felt I needed something in order to relax at home, *to chill-out*. After all, Scripture does say, "What? have ye not houses to eat and to drink in?" (*1 Corinthians 11:22a*). Isn't it amazing how we can use Scripture out of context? So I gravitated to Martell Cognac and Coca-Cola; Almost every day at least a half pint and Coca-Cola. On the holidays, I'd buy a fifth of Martell. My wife began to complain about all of the Coca-Cola bottles, so I moved them from one corner to another. I justified it to myself; at least I am not staggering or stumbling. At that time, I was a minister in The Spiritual Israel Church & Its Army. I remember my wife asking me, "What if the phone should ring one day and someone needed ministering or need you to come to assisted them? Mints don't hide that alcohol on your breath." One day I remember going into the liquor store, and the merchant had come to know me so well that he would automatically reach for the Martell before I ordered it. It bothered me, so I changed liquor stores, as if that would make a difference.

Finally, I admitted to myself that anything you feel you must have in order to relax is a problem. I was developing a dependence on liquor. I had an altar in my home. I took the last of the 1/2 a pint I had left, and I put the bottle on my altar and prayed. The influence of Satan tried to convince me that the liquor should not be on my altar. I told him, "You're *a liar!* If liquor is a problem for me that is exactly where it should be on my altar!" I prayed for three days, and finally I got my answer. The Holy Spirit told me to bury the bottle in the back yard. So, I dug a hole in the back yard, put the bottle (with the remaining liquor) into a brown plastic grocery bag (I didn't want the neighbors to see me and think I was crazy), and buried it.

Three weeks had gone by and I had totally forgotten all about what I had done. I was visiting my mother this particular day, and on my return home later that evening temptation tried to overtake me. I was driving down Seven Mile Road passing several liquor stores; it was as if the liquor signs were calling my name. I pulled over to the curb and was ready to get out of the car, when a soft voice said, "If you are going to go in there, you might as well go home and dig up the dead." A cold chill went through me. I closed my car door and shouted, "I'll be doggone if I was going to dig up the dead!" I was free! God had delivered me again. Now, I don't drink on any occasion. For me it is evil and the Scripture tells me "to eschew evil and do good" (*1 Peter 3:11*). I don't tempt myself; for me there is no such thing as drinking sociably. Even so, I was learning how to put off the old man and to put on the new. God is not through with me yet.

CHAPTER TWO
LOSING PEOPLE, PLACES, AND HOPE

James Lowe was one of my best friends. James was a year or two older than I. His father, Jack, ran an after-hour joint on 12th street. James and I would get high smoking weed (marijuana) and became two of the youngest hustlers on the set at that time. We eventually had our own joints, but the hard stuff like heroin or cocaine were off limits. We saw what heroin could do to you, and there were examples all around us. I said to myself, "That will never be me." James and I did everything together; he was my homeboy. There is a saying that smoking marijuana can lead to hard drugs. This was true for us since we had started selling barbiturates and pills like red devils, blues, etc.

I don't know when, where, or how, but James had begun snorting (*sniffing*) powdered heroin (*dope*). I don't have a clue when he started or who turned him on to it. But one day, he excitedly called me and Charles, his brother, aside. He poured out the contents of a capsule and took a snort. Then he encouraged us to take a sniff, telling us it was not the same as shooting up. I knew James, he didn't look like the addicts that I saw on the streets, he was cool, and I looked up to him like he was my brother, therefore this can't be that bad I thought to myself. I reluctantly, at the urging of my friend, indulged also. No, I don't and won't blame James for my lack of common sense. No one twisted my arm or held a gun to my head. I was not tricked or forced. In hindsight, so many times now, I wish I would have said, "NO."

Many of us, in those days, had the nerve to think that because we only snorted powdered heroin, we were better than the ones who were shooting up heroin.

There were two brothers, named Odell and OD, who were so-called pimps. Odell also sold dope. They were much older and street wise than we were. Odell had taken James under his wing and in the beginning, would set out powdered heroin for us for free. What we didn't know or realize was that he was using us to get other young people and especially young girls, to pimp them out.

Sheila was the sister of a girl I used to date. Sheila was young, full of life, and she looked up to me like a brother. She loved hanging around me and in my crowd. One day I introduced her to Odell, and he introduced her to heroin. Years later (1971) Sheila was killed in the Hazelwood massacre in Detroit. Still to this day, I feel guilty that I contributed to her loss of life by introducing her to Odell.

James and I had now migrated from snorting heroin to shooting heroin; it was overly obvious, even to us, that we were addicts. We did any and everything to get money for a fix. No one ever focuses on dying, and you live your life as though you will live forever. One day the unthinkable happened, James was stabbed to death. I thought if we could just get him to the hospital that everything would be all right. I still remember my clothes covered with his blood, and the doctor coming out and telling us that he didn't make it. My knees gave out as I sank to the floor crying as though my intestines had been ripped from me.

The police kept me locked up two to three days interrogating me. I could not sleep. In fact, the detectives wouldn't allow me to sleep. I thought I was losing my mind. They were trying to pin it on me or get me to say I knew what had happened. I needed a fix, a bath, and to get out of those clothes with James' blood on them. The detectives knew that I was young and vulnerable. If they would have kept me another day, I would have said anything that they wanted me to say just to get some sleep, but they had to release me. The detectives even came to the funeral to harass me and put me in their car. But Nathaniel, better known as Snake, opened the door and made me get out of the car. He told them that if they weren't going to charge me, to leave me alone.

No one in their right mind who watches a movie all the way through believes that there will be a different ending if they watch it a second or third time. Yet street life is lived as though it will never happen to me or I will escape its ending. Every day a new actor seeks a role or a part in the illusion. A child (girl or boy) steps on the street's stage and are transformed into the life of an adult. They are prey, and the bait are the lights, glitter, and open arm performances. There is no such word as innocence on the street's stage. There is no mama, daddy, or mercy on that stage. And the biggest enemy to that gullible youth are these words from their very own written script, "This is my life. I know what I am doing, and you can't tell me how to live my life!" How can a youth, still wet behind the ears, know anything? *And if any man think that he knoweth any thing, he knoweth nothing yet as he ought to know (1 Corinthians 8:2).*

The actors are too many to mention, such as Gunsby who was ambushed and had his brains blown out in a fur coat and fur hat while driving in a stolen Eldorado, Leddy who was simply leaning on a fence when she was killed by a man who shot into the crowd while shooting at me. Then there was Theardist, found shot to death in an alley gang-style. My cousin Ronald James, shot in the back of the head and dumped. And my cousin, May Baby, who was a very beautiful girl, sparkling and full of life. The streets and drugs stripped her of her beauty and integrity; she died of an overdose.

One time, May Baby and I had gotten into an argument because my drug money was missing. I had her boyfriend's gun in my hand trying to scare her into giving me my money, but she would not. In fact, she somewhat dared me to shoot. We were first cousins; our mothers were sisters. The gun went off, and she was shot in the arm. Even though I didn't mean to shoot her, I did. This could have resulted in horrible consequences ~ she could have died. It would have torn our family apart. She covered for me, and most of the family never knew. What matters is that I know what I did over drugs and money. No doubt someone is saying that would never have happened to them; I pray you never walk on the devil's side of the street where talk is cheap, where drugs and death have no family or age limitations. I would need pages just to tell of those I knew in their youth who were swallowed up and died from drug overdoses and murder.

It is only by God's grace that I am still here and able to write these things (the scars of my life). I know I should have been dead by my practices. I can remember practicing in the mirror how to walk looking bad and tough by imitating what I saw. Practicing looking tough (the lips and the eyes) and using words I was not taught in the church. Practicing how to hold and use a knife and gun. Yes, I was practicing to be a bad person. I was knowingly trying to cross to the dark side.

One time I got shot in the back, and my lung was pierced. I was on life support for I don't know how long. I had taken the guy's gun as we struggled and shot him. His wound was not severe. It was his brother who shot me in the back. The point is this; you can't practice getting shot. Nothing prepares you for the burning of a bullet, and feeling the life leave your body as you gasp for air and fade into unconsciousness. Nothing prepares you for feeling the tears of your mother on your face as you slip in and out of consciousness in the bright lights of the critical care unit of the hospital. Even so when I was released, I returned to the stage of Seward and 12th Street. I still didn't know the significance of the song, *Somebody prayed for me, had me on their mind, took the time and prayed for me.*

I remember sneaking and shooting up in the bathroom at my aunt and grandmother's apartment. I overdosed (OD'ed) and they called the EMS. They had also called my mother. As I was gaining consciousness, somebody was beating on me and crying. It was my mother. It was tearing her apart. The EMS had to pull her off me. I didn't realize how you drag those that love you through the nightmare of the street stage that you chose. Yet, I have said, "I'm not hurting nobody but myself."

When I joined The Spiritual Israel Church & Its Army and God delivered me, I tried to go back and talk to others in the streets about what God had done and was doing for me. Some wanted to say that I had always been lucky and wanted to talk about when I had money, cars, and this or that. Perhaps they even thought that this was just another hustle. But I knew that it was not luck; that I could not save myself; and that every time I tried it on my own I fell deeper and deeper. I lost count of how many times I had said, *"When **I** get myself together."* I was unaware of Jesus words, "...Without me ye can do nothing *(John 15: 1-5)."*

My family and friends didn't know how many times I cried and screamed in the horror of the life I had created on the street's stage. They were still living in a superficial past that no longer existed for me. "Lord, how could I make them see," I asked. In fact, my life is like a book that appears fictional even to me. But only God and I know that the pages are true, and that it was He that saved a wretch like me. *O wretched man that I am! who shall deliver me from the body of this death? (Romans 7:24)* Not because I am better than any of them, in fact I am probably even worse; the chief of sinners (*1 Timothy 1:15*). All I know is that I cried and I cried and He heard my cry (*Psalm 18:6*). He delivered me from myself. At the time, that was the only hell I knew. I didn't have the Biblical understanding of hell, but I believe that if He saved me, He can save anybody.

Sometimes I think about the ones I went back to give a testimony; many are no longer here. What if they would have only given God a try? Even so, God has chosen to keep me here for His purpose.

CHAPTER THREE
TRUST GOD (DEPENDING ON MOTHER ROSE)

Bishop Bride Mother Rose Alice Tumpkin was her title and name in The Spiritual Israel Church & Its Army. She was the co-pastor with Elder William Carnegie at Temple #8 where I joined and attended service. It was her words that I had remembered the first time Snake, had brought me there on 24th Street. She was a strong-willed woman who said what she meant and stood on what she said. Even the men stood still when she spoke whether they liked it or not. Many who did not really know her said she was mean and didn't like her sharp way of speaking, which many times was like an order. Her husband had been the King of Israel before he died (many years before I joined). We'll get to the doctrine of the church later.

Mother Rose had taken me as one of her spiritual sons in the church and many believed that I was her favorite. I could talk to her about anything, such as my past, things I had done, and was doing. She never sugar-coated things or condemned me. She made herself available to me 24/7. She told me no matter what time of the night, if I had a problem to call her. I studied Israel's doctrine under her. She would always tell me, "Robert, you don't have enough patience." As time moved on thinking that I had grown, I would always ask her, "Mother Rose, do I have enough patience yet?" She would always reply, "No!"

At that time, I was still smoking weed and was still in the pill hustle. I had come to the church just as I was. I didn't pretend, and I didn't lie about it. This is not a justification, but just the plain hard truth. Mother Rose neither condoned my behavior nor condemned my lifestyle. She never said or told me to stop. I think she knew that if she had told me to do that, I couldn't at that time. What she said to me was, "Robert just like you were successful in the streets, you can be successful in God." Of course, I didn't know what she meant at that time. She would tell me that I needed to learn to have faith in the God of Israel. She would give me Scriptures to read, and she instructed me to get a notebook and write out my thoughts and my talking with God. Her favorite saying was, "This may be a woman's body, but these are a man's words."

When I would ask for advice, she would always tell me that she had to pray and see what the God of Israel would give her to give to me. Here, was where I saw the weakness of my patience because I'd want a quick answer. But you didn't hurry Mother Rose, so I'd wait – impatiently.

As time went on, and the more I learned, I stopped hustling altogether. But I had money, and it was easy to praise God when you had money and things seemed to be going well. Mother Rose told me Robert, "You may have to lose everything you have acquired from the streets to learn to trust God and have faith in Him."

Hearing it was one thing, but having it happen to you was another. I told Mother Rose that I wanted to do something different, but I didn't know how. All I knew how to do was to hustle the streets. I had done this from youth. In fact, the only time I would ever even get a job was to work long enough to get enough money to get into another hustle, and then I would quit. I had lost jobs at Ford, Chrysler, and you name it, always with the same results. I had squandered so many opportunities because I didn't have the intention of doing what was right. By that time, I was in my thirties.

Once again I heard these words from her, "Let me pray and see what the God of Israel would give me to give to you." Impatiently, I waited. After about a week or two, Mother Rose said, "The God of Israel told me to tell you to go back to school." "What?" I said. "School? But I'm in my thirties." This was not what I wanted to hear.

But I had learned to trust in her words and instructions. I was still leaning on her faith because mine was weak, if I had any at all. I remember Mother Rose once telling me that the reasons I was missing my blessings was because I was always hanging out and at someone else's house (women). She said, I could not get my blessings because I was always in the streets and would never stay at home. Long story short: A lady friend had asked me to come over that night. Like a fool, I told her what Mother Rose had said. With her hands on her hips she scoffed and asked, "You do everything Mother Rose says?" I didn't reply.

Late that evening I was out riding my motorcycle on a summer night. I started to go over to the lady friend's house but thought about what Mother Rose had said to me, so I went home instead. I parked my motorcycle up in the yard in the front of my car that was in my driveway. I went into the house, took off my clothes, got a bowl of ice cream, sat down, and turned on the TV. I heard a noise but didn't think much of it, but I got up to peek out of the window. There in my car was a head moving. I startled a thief and he startled me. Other than my door there was no damage. I said out loud as if the lady friend could hear me, "You dog-gone right; I do what Mother Rose tell me." If I had not come home, my car would have been stolen.

GOING BACK TO SCHOOL:

I attended Adult Education School and obtained my G.E.D. certificate. In 1982, I enrolled at Wayne County Community College (WC3) after speaking with a counselor there. I wanted to learn about and open my own computer repair service. At that time there were none in the black neighborhoods. The counselor asked, "How are you going to fix them if you don't know what computers do?" That made sense to me, so I enrolled in Computer and Data Processing. I learned about what computers did and how to program in various computer languages. I loved programing and became a Computer Lab Assistant.

For two years, at the beginning of each new class, the instructor would ask the students to stand and give their name and field of study. No one ever told me that I was on the wrong path and that learning how to fix computers was a different two-year degree. I needed and took advantage of the various tutoring sessions in mathematics, algebra, English, etc. I would be at WC3 early in the morning until closing in the evening. It was as if there was only time for church and school. It would be remiss of me not to acknowledge all the help I had along the way. Both in college as well as the church. There were many people that God sent my way to help me, at no charge. My money had long ago run out.

I was attending college on financial grants, was now on food stamps, and received a minimal social service check which was not enough to pay my rent. I could not pay car insurance. I was seeing the downward spiral. In my mind, I started thinking about hustling again. I told Mother Rose that I was thinking of dropping out of school and why. She hit the ceiling. *"You are going to school if I have to come and sit on the steps with you,"* she said. I remember thinking, who is this 77-year-old lady talking to me like this? Needless to say, I heard her and she persevered with me.

No, a bag of money didn't fall out of the sky and solve my woes. But God made a way. My landlady, Mrs. Kelly, owned several houses on the block where I lived. She agreed to let me paint for her to offset the rent while going to school. All I can say is that I tried, but I knew nothing at all about painting. So she let me out of that. Yet she did not evict me. I can't explain it, but she showed me mercy.

I no longer had car insurance, but I was still driving my car to get to church and to school. One evening I was backing out of the driveway on my way to church, and I was not paying attention. I backed into my neighbor's car on the other side of the street. He came out and boy was he hot. I could see that he was refraining himself, but even so, he told me to go and don't worry about it. He would take care of it.

I was on my way to school one day and did a rolling-stop at the stop sign. The police pulled me over. The lady officer looked on the back seat in my car and saw a bunch of school books. "You attending school?" she asked. "Yes," I replied. She said, "You can't afford to pay any tickets going to school." They let me go.

I am not promoting that anyone do what I did. I am just reporting that God had mercy on me, provided for me, and made ways out of situations for me.

I lived there at the house I was renting from Mrs. Kelly (when I could pay) until shortly after I graduated July, 1984. Then I got a job that relocated me to Illinois.

GRADUATING WITH HONORS FROM WC3:

I graduated with an Associate Degree of Applied Science in Computer and Data Processing with Honor, "cum laude," from Wayne County Community College (WC3). The funny thing was that I had never heard of cum laude and didn't know what it meant.

Mother Rose asked me smiling, "Now aren't you glad that I didn't let you give up and quit school?" I just grinned back at her. My real Mother and my fiancé attended the ceremony. My only problem was now what do I do; what is next? It seemed like after two years of all that hard work I should have more than a piece of paper.

It wasn't until I was applying for entry at Lawrence Technological University that I found out that I had obtained a degree in the wrong area. The counselor said, "I'm sorry Mr. Anderson, you would only have *another* two-year degree if you pursued this curriculum." I was a little disappointed, but it was too late now. Besides I had really gotten into the programing aspect of computers. So I applied and enrolled for a four-year degree at MaryGrove College. While there, I continued to work, the minimal hours, as a Computer Lab Assistant at WC3

AT&T sent recruitment representatives to WC3. I had several outstanding reference letters from those I had worked for at WC3 as a lab assistant and tutor. I was interviewed and accepted. But all those recruited would need to fly to Chicago for a physical examination. "Oh Lord," I cried, "What am I going to do? If I take a physical, they are going to know about my past. They are going to see the tracks and scars from years of drug abuse." I called Mother Rose detailing my fears. The only thing she said was, "Robert don't worry about it."

HIRED BY AT&T AND MARRIED:

I called the number I was given related to the examination from a pay phone at school. I thought I was calling for a scheduled appointment. Instead the voice on the other end said, "No you don't have to come here for the physical and it can be taken over the phone by answering a series of questions." None of the questions asked were related to drug usage or things of my past. I passed! When I hung-up the phone, I shouted and jumped for joy. I could not wait to give Mother Rose the good news. I asked the others who were recruited, and it appeared that I was the only one who took the examination over the phone; everyone else flew to Chicago for their physicals. I was learning what God could do; but unknowingly I was still depending on the faith of Mother Rose. If she said it, I believed it.

I got married in May of 1985 and left for Chicago to start work at AT&T in Naperville IL on June 3, 1985. AT&T paid to relocate me to Illinois and for the storage of my furniture until I found a place. The plan was that my wife, Jo Ann, would eventually transfer through her job to come there.

However, we commuted back and forth just shy of five years. The Spiritual Israel Church & Its Army had various temples around the states. One of the ministers in Chicago, Reverend Jan Tate, was very kind and allowed me to move in with him until I secured an apartment in the suburb where I would be working. I attended the temple that he attended, but there was a minor problem for me, and I was confused. They were teaching and singing about Jesus and not just the God of Israel as I had heard at my local Church back in Detroit and other temples that I had attended around the states. I will provide more on the doctrine of The Spiritual Israel Church & Its Army later.

FEAR OF OPENING MY MOUTH, GIVING GOD THE PRAISE:

One day my supervisor, Dan, said to me, "Robert almost every other week you are on the road traveling back and forth to Detroit, and yet you get your work done, and you're always on time. With your family in Detroit it must be hard on you. How do you do it?" he asked.

I wanted to tell him it was God that was making a way for me and the road was easy, but at first my mouth would not move. I thought to myself, how do you talk about God in the corporate world? Was I ashamed to talk about God in this place and share that without Him I would not be? I did not want to say it, but finally I said, "It is the God of Israel who makes the way easy for me and I could not make it without Him." I never spoke to him about the subject again and in fact I had several other supervisors after him. About four years later as I was preparing to relocate back to Detroit, I ran into my old supervisor, Dan. He wished me well and told me that his wife had passed with Cancer. He said when he was going through the experience of her illness and death that he had thought about me and what I had said. **"What you said about your faith in God was what helped me through,"** he said. A cold chill went through me, and I could have hit the floor. All I could remember was how I did not want to say anything, how I did not want to mention God in the Corporate world. I was learning never be ashamed to open my mouth about God. "Whosoever therefore shall confess me before men, him will I confess also before my Father which is in heaven." (Matthew 10:32)

GOD BREAKS DOWN MY SKIN COLOR BARRIERS:

My worldview was limited to what I had seen in the streets and somewhat shaped by the teachings of The Spiritual Israel Church & Its Army. Because of some experiences from my past, I still unknowingly had biases that were about to be challenged. For one, I was the only black among my coworkers on the various teams that I was assigned to in the work place at AT&T in Naperville IL. But I could not tell it by the way they treated me and made me a part of the team. When I had graduated, I thought I was hot stuff in programming; I was about to find out how little I knew. There were documentations that had to be written, testing, and more documents. All these documents had to be approved and signed off on by those on the team. Remember, using tutors I had squeezed through college, but I was now in the real world, and no one has to help you do anything.

However, I shared an office with a Caucasian woman named Laura. If I remember correctly, she was also assigned to the same team. Evidently while going over my documents, she picked up that I still had a lot of problems including punctuation, spelling, flow, and you name it. "Do you mind if I would markup your documents before you turned them in?" she asked. "No, I don't mind," I replied. My God, when she gave the documents back to me there were red marks, corrections, and suggestions all over the papers. Because of Laura, the white lady, I learned and improved. No longer could I make the statement that white people won't help you.

Yes, I had to put the work in, but those people there helped me. I learned from others as well about testing, programing, etc. I never received a bad rating at review time, I was being promoted and received raises in pay.

We had a black affirmative action group and the Black Heritage group at the company, and I attended regular meetings. When other blacks would complain about some of their experiences or issues, I could never relate because I had different experiences. It was like God had me covered. If I would have said anything to the contrary, it would have been a lie. The supervisor would sometimes tell me, "Bob I see you've been working late and that all your work is in order. You don't have to rush back Monday morning because I know you get your work done." He knew I was commuting back and forth to Detroit. I would leave out late Friday night and rush back in time to start work on Monday mornings. I had the routine down to a tee; God and me.

I met people that I thought were black, many who were darker than me, only to learn that they were from India or other countries. I was having culture shock. I was a long way from 12th street. AT&T was a very diverse work place. This was just the beginning of my eye-opening experiences.

GOD OPENS ANOTHER DOOR AND BRINGS ME BACK TO DETROIT:

After about four years in Illinois, I began to miss Detroit where most my family lived. If I could transfer with AT&T back to Michigan, my wife and I would no longer have to commute back and forth. AT&T had a project going where they were trying to move many in the work force around the country into sales. I thought perhaps this is my chance, although I didn't know anything about sales other than my previous street life. So how hard could this be?

I talked to my supervisor who was very supportive. The managers loaned me out to another AT&T office in Illinois so I could acquire experience working with the sales force. I was signed up for the sales training where you had to take several tests and did sales role-play.

I had interviewed with Ben Serzo, who was an AT&T manager back in Southfield, Michigan. I had several recommendation letters from my various supervisors and from the people at the AT&T sales office in Illinois. In my mind, I was ready. But we had to wait on the outcome of the sales training I was attending. I had talked with… yes, you know who, Mother Rose, and all my things were boxed and ready to go.

I got a letter from AT&T regretfully informing me that I didn't qualify for the sales project that was being rolled out. My heart dropped, hit the floor, and I was devastated. Once again, I called Mother Rose, asking what I was going to do. She told me to leave my bags and boxes packed. I called Ben Serzo and informed him of the letter I'd received from AT&T sales. He said cursing, "I don't care what they said, they don't know their head from a horse's #$%, I want YOU ANYWAY." Ben assured me that he would start the necessary paperwork to transfer me. When I got off the phone, I was jumping, shouting, and praising God. Once again God was showing me that it was not about my degrees or who I was. Without Him I could do nothing. But it was He that opened doors for me (*Revelation 3:7-8*). I was learning to have faith (Luke 17:5), but was not yet weaned from Mother Rose's faith in God. God was still working on me. I rented a U-haul, loaded all my things, and I was off to Detroit, Michigan. By now you may have noticed that during these times the name of Jesus is hardly mentioned in my writing. This is because of the teaching I was under at that time in The Spiritual Israel Church & Its Army, where we were taught to call God by His name, "The God of Israel." While they talked about Jesus, it was from the position that He had finished His work, using John 17:4 out of context. More on this later...

I started working for Ben Serzo at the AT&T Southfield office in about 1989 as a technical consultant working with those responsible for sales. Ben managed the sales force that served the Big 3 automobiles dealers, GM, Ford, and Chrysler in the Michigan area.

My job supported sales, and sometimes I was responsible for software installations and ensuring computers were setup and problems resolved. I was supposed to call the hotline who would guide you through different scenarios when there were issues. I quickly learned that many of the hotline people didn't know as much as I did. They were reading manuals, and if it was not on the page, they would be lost. I could read!

FINALLY, I GET TO FIX SOME COMPUTERS:

If you recall, my goal was to learn how to repair computers. That was why I attended college at WC3, but I earned a degree in the wrong curriculum. So, I didn't learn computer repair while attending college. Here it was, five to six years later, and I'm downtown at the Renaissance Center Building with computer parts all over the floor at 3:00 a.m. in the morning. This is where I begin to learn about computers, no one taught me. I would read the manuals, it took time, but thank God I got it. What I didn't know was that AT&T Managers weren't supposed to be doing union related work. As a manager, I was violating the union skilled labor contract. I was unaware of this oversight. The proper procedure was to open a ticket and have the work done by union labor personnel. But God has a sense of humor. By the time it caught up with me, it was too late. I had been working on and repairing computers for so long that I became somewhat good at what I was doing.

I was at a Ford car dealership in Dearborn working on a computer one day, and a PBX technician, Paul Swan, was dispatched there to resolve a PBX phone switch issue that the dealership was experiencing. We talked, trading general conversation, as he worked on the PBX, and I repaired the computer. Later, when I returned to the Southfield office, Ben informed me that a grievance had been written up on me for working on a computer. It turned out, to my surprise, Paul was a union steward. He did what he was supposed to do (I just didn't let him catch me anymore). Later, Paul and I would often laugh about it.

An opportunity came about for a position where I would have been working for another manager, Pete Foxe. I would be over three districts: Michigan, Indiana, and Milwaukee; and responsible for terminal controllers. This was a dream come true position, I would be moving up I thought. I interviewed with Pete Foxe and supposedly got the job. Ben was waiting on the paperwork so he could also replace me. Weeks went by, finally we heard from Pete that he had decided to hire someone else for the position. Of course, I felt let down, but it didn't last long. About a week later, AT&T sold off those controllers and all those folks under Pete Foxe no longer had a job. Here I was jumping, shouting, and praising God again; not at what had happened to them, but at what God had kept from happening to me. He knows what is best for us. He knows what is around the corner. I was loving and learning this walk with God. I could not understand why I had been so foolish in all my years, and what had taken me so long to turn to God?

Ben and I had a great working relationship. He got a new position in Ann Arbor at AT&T College & University Systems (ACUS). I made it known to him that if there was a position there under him, I was interested. God is good because there was.

After Ben left, I was working under another manager, Tony. He was not a bad manager, but he was not Ben. I learned that he was upset with me because I was TOO happy that I was going to work for Ben in the Ann Arbor office at ACUS. Shortly after I left, AT&T closed that Southfield office, and many of those employees had to find jobs where possible in AT&T. My point is that at every step God kept me in a way that He would get the glory; showing what He can do with a used up, worn out, and good for nothing dope addict. I learned that it is not over until God says it is over. He has mercy on whom He will.

TRAVELING THE COUNTRY AT THE COMPANY'S EXPENSE:

ACUS was the candy shop of all my learning. There I was responsible for purchasing computers, and I could build them as I chose for specific functions without the hassle of the union. In fact, I even worked with union technicians on sites. It always amazes me how God can turn things around. I was responsible for installing and maintaining computers at various colleges and universities around the country. A co-worker and I wrote/developed the software that was key to AT&T ACUS collecting the call data from PBX switches, polling the data, and making the call data available for billing. These systems and my responsibilities were later rolled over to Military bases. It was during this time that I got to travel all over the states and see things that I never thought I would get to see.

Sometimes, I would make a vacation for my wife and I, out of my work-related travels, after all my expenses were fully paid. I simply paid for my wife's expenses. Many times, I took advantage of my accumulated Frequent Flyer Miles to cover her fare.

I used to laugh wondering what my neighbors thought I was doing. Limo service would pick me up and drop me off; in a day or two I was repeating the cycle. Maybe because of my past, I could have thought that person has got to be doing something wrong. But with each experience, I just could not get over what God was doing in my life.

If our church was having a convention in some state, I was always able to attend, and there were several during the year. If I didn't have a work project that needed my attention near the church location, I'd take a class related to my work and field. I learned how to kill two birds with one stone, I enjoyed it, and gave God the glory. I did it all within the guidelines of AT&T's code of conduct.

God had brought me a long way from nodding and scratching, slipping in and out of consciousness, high on drugs, a junkie on a street corner. He had taught me how to use my mind and hands for things other than committing crimes against society and self-destruction.

I loved my work because God had given me something I could do and do well. I had no problem working and putting in extra hours long after everyone else had gone home. I was always trying to figure out how I could make things better; it was a game to me, but a game that I took serious. The only thing I didn't do was put my work before attending my church services; I was serious about church. On a time or two I had to make that known. Of course, AT&T later clamped down on working hours not reported because it is against the law, and they could be fined or sued. In fact, you could be disciplined for working outside of your hours, but I never was.

MY FIRST BUSINESS VENTURE:

I started my first business, Computer Wizard. I would repair folk's computers, setup networks, and install software. I also provided tutorial services. It was great for a while, but there was something about folks not wanting to pay for the skills that reside in a person's head that I just don't get. Especially if it only takes you ten or twenty minutes to do it.

So, I phased out of that business, except for special projects that I under took for extra money.

I cannot express enough in words to show the doors that God opened for me being at ACUS. Even when some thought to setup road blocks for me, God used them for my good. The skills that I learned were usable for the church in so many ways. It was not just about me, but the church will always be a beneficiary of what God has performed in my life. I owe it all to my Lord and Savior, Jesus Christ.

GRADUATING WITH HONORS FROM DCB:

In August, 1991, while working at ACUS, I obtained the Degree of Bachelor of Business Administration (cum laude) from Detroit College of Business (DCB) ~ now known as Davenport University.

RETIRED FROM AT&T:

I retired from AT&T in 2013. No one could ever have told me that I would have retired from anywhere, or be alive because of the way I had lived my life. In my case, I know I was guilty; I know I didn't do anything to warrant mercy. I know I squandered 2nd, 3rd, and how ever many chances. Like Naaman, I can say I know that there is God.

> **2 Kings 5:15** And he returned to the man of God, he and all his company, and came, and stood before him: and he said, Behold, now I know that there is no God in all the earth, but in Israel: now therefore, I pray thee, take a blessing of thy servant.

And God has revealed Himself to us in the person of His Son Jesus Christ. (John 1:18, Hebrews 1:2)

CHAPTER FOUR
DON'T DEPEND ON SELF (PROVERBS 3:5)

Have you ever been walking down the street and accidently walked into a pole or in the house and walked into a door? Once? Twice? After a while it gets to be old news, and you know that something is not clicking.

PRISON:

I went to prison for robbing a dope house in 1967. Actually, I pleaded guilty to Attempted Robbery. I was with two adults. They told the Judge that I was just with them but didn't do anything. The guy who was robbed told the Judge the same thing, yet I was sentenced one to two years. I served eighteen months and was released for good behavior. Believe it or not, the adults got probation. I believe, because of my past and my juvenile record, that the Judge was trying to teach me a lesson and perhaps even save my life. I went through Jackson Prison to a minimal security camp. But I did not change; I was not rehabilitated. It is easy to say what you are not going to do confined in a rectangular box where you can't get out, and your old habits can't get in. I was convicted; I was a convict, but I had no conviction within my heart because prison is not God. Yes, I was sorry, but not for my actions, but sorry that I got caught and could not wiggle and squirm my way out of it.

FIRST MARRIAGE:

I had previously married a woman called Bea, who was ten years older than I. I had met Bea, a bartender on 12th street, during the days when James and I ran after-hour joints. When the bar would close, the crowd would follow her to our joint. She told me I was too young, but I think it intrigued her that a young (18-19-year-old) man was infatuated with her. My nose was wide open and I was like a puppet. I was now in another league with access to a different clientele. But with Bea, I was also out of my league, school was in session, and I didn't listen to my mother who tried to warn me. I knew what I wanted ~ I thought. Needless to say, that in my kind of lifestyle everything that goes up ~ must come down. I filed for a divorce after years of separation. Even a puppet grows up.

The only person who came to visit me or wrote to me while I was incarcerated was my mother. I hated it when she would ask me if I had I heard from Bea. "No," I replied and would give some excuse. My mother would cry, and I'd promised that I was going to do better next time around. I was going to change. Inside four walls, you actually believe the lie that you are telling yourself, but there was the illusion waiting out there for me. I would walk; no, run right back to it.

It was Bea and Snake who picked me up after I was released. It was easy to say what you won't do while confined to a square cubical with no way out. Things were not the same, but I played the part.

> **Luke 11:24-26** When the unclean spirit is gone out of a man, he walketh through dry places, seeking rest; and finding none, he saith, I will return unto my house whence I came out. And when he cometh, he findeth it swept and garnished. Then goeth he, and taketh to him seven other spirits more wicked than himself; and they enter in, and dwell there: and the last state of that man is worse than the first.

You quickly learn that the world doesn't stand still while you are incarcerated. Neither do the streets. Soon, I was back to selling and using drugs.

SHORT LIVED STREET FAME AND CROOKED POLICE:

Let's just say, street wise, I began to hit pay dirt. Everybody wanted my stuff. In no way am I bragging about what I did or mean to glorify that life, far from it. But I am hopeful that it will reveal the consequences of this type of lifestyle, and what happens to one who sells his soul. Yes, I thought I was the man; I was outsmarting the Police. When they had me, they didn't have me. Because of my youthful looks, they thought I was just one of his (my) junkie workers. They would let me go. The Big Four and Stress Unit would raid the dope house and never find any drugs or money because of ingenious hiding places that I had built. I would tell them we were waiting on Bobby Morris (myself) to bring the stuff, and then I would pretend to be sick and needing a fix. I would have a little money in my sock and they (the police) would take that.

My problem with the police started when I got flashy, and they realized who I was really. I had extravagant clothes, cars, houses, jewelry, furs, money and more money. If I would have ventured out of my 16-block radius, I would have been a nobody. Here, even though I was pushing dope, I would stop the ice cream truck and buy all the kids ice cream as if I had done some great thing. They knew me by name. I had a 16-block radius of fame.

In my mind, the police were supposed to be honest, upstanding, and law-abiding. They were supposed to be everything that didn't apply to me. But the love of money even touches some in police uniforms. I didn't know it at the time, but some of these Stress units were involved in drugs. They would raid dope houses in one area, keep most of the dope and money, but still arrest and charge the person with possession. They would take the rest of the dope to be sold by their partners who ran dope houses in the Pingree and 12th street area.

Their big problem was that they could never catch me with drugs. So they would carry me to various locations and beat me up. But I would refuse to pay them off or give them any information. One time they beat me so bad that my head was swollen like a basketball, I could hardly see, and was bloody. People took pity and attempted to take me to the hospital, but the Big Four Police unit backed-up, and made them leave me be.

Who do you tell when you are a criminal yourself, and the police in the neighborhood are bigger criminals than you? Plus, I lived by the code of the streets; I was not a snitch. After a while, they would wait hoping to spot me. They'd pull me over and arrest me claiming that they had busted me at my dope house with dope in my pocket. I was no longer out smarting the police. I was paying a lot of money in lawyer and bail bond fees and with blood.

I remember the Goldfarb Bail Bondsman that tried to give me some financial advice, but it went totally over my head. "Look at you," he said. (I was dressed like super-fly). "Your fancy clothes and cars are drawing attention to you. Learn to invest your money," he said. I looked at him and laughed; he was wearing straight leg pants and loafers. "You can't tell me how to dress," I said arrogantly. "You're right," he said, "But that is why you are paying me to bond you and your crew out of jail, and my money is in the bank." It would be far too late when I finally understood what he was trying to tell me. I was good at outsmarting myself.

After one such beating, I happened to run into one of the off-duty Stress Officers at a Kentucky Fried Chicken near where I was living. Bad for him, he approached me; he didn't have the others with him, and I was not afraid of him. About a week later the unit picked me up, but he was not with them. They forced me down on the floor in the back of the squad car and were driving around while beating me. They were trying to locate the officer, but they couldn't reach him. They said he had told them I tried to run him down with my car. After a while, they kicked me out of the squad car. After that, I started riding around with a shotgun in my car; I was tired of them beating me. I had made up my mind that the next time they stopped me I was going to use it. I had heard that they had a contract out on me. I knew that I could not win, it no longer mattered to me, and I did not think about dying. I didn't know it, but somebody was praying for me. Later in my life, my mother would tell me how she had asked the church to pray for me.

I remember a so-called prophet over on 12th street once telling me that if I didn't change my ways, I'd be dead before I reached the age of twenty-one. I had laughed at him because he had one of his hands all bandaged up, but he was talking about healing people and prophesying to them. Laughing, I mocked him and said, "If you can heal everybody else, why don't you heal your own hand?" He began to read me. He told me things about myself and what was happening in my life. There was no way he could have known. I had never met him before that day. He put fear in me, I was no longer laughing, but even so, my life didn't change.

Due to a drug drought, I became very insignificant, and I began to spiral down again. Sometime afterward there was an interesting sting: police were arrested with certain drug dealers from the Pingree area [*The 10th Precinct Conspiracy Trial*].[1] It made the news and television. When they were found guilty one of the crooked cops, that had beat me up, was on television crying real tears, saying he hadn't done anything wrong. It was not until years later that I understood the events as they unfolded. Clearly, what I was doing was evil, I was evil, and God used someone that was wicked like me to buffet me. The righteous won't lie and dirty their hands. "The LORD hath made all things for himself: yea, even

---

[1] http://freeingjohnsinclair.aadl.org/node/200055. Retrieved September 15, 2016

the wicked for the day of evil." (*Proverbs 16:4*) I just thank God that He didn't allow them to take my life.

CHAPTER FIVE
BROKEN CONNECTIONS

Every day we would end-up at Corinne's (Big-Mama) house, day-in and day-out. It was like a-merry-go-round. Everything flowed through Big-Mama house. We would sit around the kitchen table getting high and talking about what we were going to do. The next day we were right back doing the same thing all over again. It was as if the cycle could not be broken. Money or no money all were on this merry-go-round. When I started attending The Spiritual Israel Church & Its Army, it was like God was taking me off that merry-go-round. Even so, I tried to resist because I was comfortable there, and I had ties there. But that was about to change. When I started to go to school, there was no time for Big-Mama's house. I got more involved in the church, I wanted to talk church (God) with them, but they didn't want what I wanted. I didn't understand this. It didn't help that at that time I still smoked weed with them and wanted to talk about God. I didn't understand that God was pulling on me (there was a war going on within me). I thought I could maintain the old relationships, and even though now attending Church, I told myself weed was not bad. At least I was not shooting dope. The old man in me did not want to die. I didn't want them to think I thought I was better than anybody, but I no longer wanted to be who I was. That person had let me down so many times, and yet he did not want to die.

The pill business was good, but even so, the more I attended church the harder it became for me to justify what I was doing. I needed someone to tell me, "You are wrong." For someone to tell me to "STOP." But it never came from another person; there was no crutch. I played over and over in my mind all the times I had been up and each time I fell, I fell lower and lower. So many times I had people patting me on the back because I had money and on the block street fame, but when I fell, they let me know what they really thought about me. I was nothing and nobody. I tried living by the code and never snitched to get out of a jam. I was naïve enough to believe the code. But over time I saw people that I admired and looked up to that were rough and tough, some murderers, who dropped the code when they were facing stiff charges. Home boys snitched on home boys if it meant saving themselves. The street code was a myth, and I was its fool. I knew I never wanted to go back to that place in life again. In fact, I don't think I would make it if it happened again. "Lord, I want out," I cried from inside of myself, but even so I put on the front for all my so-called business friends and everyone else. It was like I was playing a part in a play; a place that I didn't want to be. But I kept going to church.

GOD PULLS ME OFF THE MERRY-GO-ROUND:

One day a lady customer came to the door for some pills; she had a baby in her arms and wanted to trade her baby formula and food for some pills. That did it! It was hypocritical for me to believe that I could go to church and praise God for delivering me from the poison of the streets, and then turn around and sell that same poison to someone else – destroying lives. The money no longer justified my rationalization. I didn't know or have the slightest idea what I was going to do, but I knew that day I could no longer do this. My heart was finally convicted: how could I say I love God who delivered me and then sell death to someone else?

I tried to talk to my friends about it. They called me Doc because of my so-called illegal business enterprise. "Doc," they said, "How are you just going to shut down, and what are you going to do?" They thought I was joking or out of my mind because all I talked about was church and God. I know they no doubt hated to see me coming. I know it was out of place, but I remember it was like I could not help myself; I could not stop talking about God. As hypocritical as it was, He was pulling on me. There was a war going on inside me.

The Spiritual Israel Church & Its Army General Assembly was being held in New York that year. It was the first assembly that I would attend there. I reasoned with myself and told Star, my girlfriend at that time who ran my business, that I was closing down the business. Star attended the church with me once or twice, and in time she moved on. I was learning that everyone doesn't want what you want in life.

After that, I really became zealous in the doctrine of The Spiritual Israel Church & Its Army, and it began to pull me away from the life and those I thought I could not live without: family, friends, and foes.

GOD RELOCATES ME TO BREAK ALL TIES:

God has a sense of humor. After graduating, AT&T recruited me and relocated me to Naperville, Illinois (outside of Chicago). I was there for almost five years. It was like God was making sure all ties with my former life were broken. When I returned, I didn't know where anyone was. Some had died, some were in jail, and some I have no clue what happened to them. But I do remember going over to where Big Mama lived. Something should have registered when I saw the front of the house, but it didn't. I went in and came out as fast as I had gone in. Somewhere along the timeline Big Mama had gotten into using crack. She was no longer Big Mama. I could not bring myself to look at her, the house, or the people that were around the table – they were on the same merry-go-round that God had reached over and snatched me off. I made some quick excuse and hurriedly left. I never saw her again until some years later when I attended her funeral. But I often think, "Why me? Lord you saved me?" I tried to tell them about God the best I knew how, and surely God loved them the same as He loved me? I know I was no better and perhaps even worse than many of them, perhaps the chief of sinners. I believe God gives us all a tug, but I believe we must reach for Him and He will take our hand. I am reminded of the Scripture "…if I make my bed in hell, behold, thou art there." (*Psalm 139:8b*)

CHAPTER SIX
IT'S NOT ABOUT ME

I think about Mother Rose's words; she would tell me, "Robert, you can be just as successful in God as you were in the world." But I'm learning that after so-called success, then what? Men die, whether of the world or of the church. No one can take earthly success to their grave. Others may get the benefit of it or squander it. Success is like a child's toy. After you get the toy, you want another. You soon digress; it has no lasting joy.

GOD GIVES ME A BUSINESS IDEA:

In 1998, one night after working twelve or more hours at the AT&T office in Ann Arbor, I left work about 2:00 a.m. in the morning heading home on M14 East. I was so tired that I could hardly keep my eyes open, and I could not wait to jump into my bed. The radio was on and the weirdest song was playing that didn't make any sense. At first I was not paying any attention, and then I heard the words something about "The Gun in My Hand with the Can...." "What in the world is this song talking about?" I asked myself. What I heard didn't make any sense. But then I heard the Holy Spirit say to me, "Why don't you go home and write something positive?" Now remember I was dead tired, but as soon as I got home, I immediately sat down at my computer and created a design composing a short poem:

TODAY, I Know Who I Am.

For My IMAGE Is Strong in The Eyes of The Beholder.

My DESTINY Though Peaceful Causes the World To fear ME.

I SHALL Break All Chains From My MIND That Hinder Me.

And My Actions SHALL Shout!

I Am the BLACK MAN.

At that time, I didn't own any other equipment to start a business. I purchased some t-shirts and sweat-shirts, and I took my design to A&D Embroidery for them to silk screen my shirts. They were very helpful, and we worked out reasonable pricing that would allow me to make a small profit.

I took my shirt project to the church and worked out a plan where the church would get a donation from my sales there. People took orders for me at Ford and Chrysler factories, USPS facilities, and you name it. My wife, Jo Ann, was taking orders at work and from family. People helped me build my business. I designed other t-shirts. I took orders to apply photos on t-shirts and coffee mugs. As I began to make money, I would turn it over into purchasing equipment and supplies, investing in my new business venture. My mother was my biggest supporter. "My son this, and my son does that," she would say. She would take orders at her church, and I got projects from there as well. At Christmas and birthdays, it was my products she purchased to give as presents. We all wore my designs, that was the best advertisement. People would inquire as to where and how could they purchase it!

BRANCHING OUT – NEW VENTURES

I soon learned that I needed to know something about photography to increase my profits and to ensure that I didn't have copyright issues using other people's work. I took photography classes and in my spare time did photography in nightclubs. Big Jim, a friend and member of the church, was a professional wedding photographer who took me under his wing. He taught me wedding photography and videography. It wasn't long before he was sending me out on wedding jobs by myself. I already knew the computer expertise using Photoshop and other Adobe software packages. Everything I was learning was adding to, enhancing, and supporting other aspects of my business.

I would look for AT&T classes that I could take in New York. Since that covered my expenses, for also attending trade shows, it allowed me to go to New York China Town outlets looking for the unusual and different items that I felt people would love. One example was women's silk scarves. I could not keep enough of them. I didn't make or design them, but they were bought at a reasonable low cost and then resold which allowed for a big but reasonable profit. Another example was shirt designs with photos of Afro-Americans who had made contributions or that were leaders in the struggle of black people. These sold even after black history month.

If you are my age, you may recall Taystee Bread. They had a slogan, "Baked While You Sleep.™"[2] I wanted this same mindset. While others were sleeping, I was trying to bake the next business idea. A pastor in Spiritual Israel once gave us this analogy: "The farmer plants seeds, and then he put a scarecrow in the field to scare off the crows. But the crows still eat the seeds of the field, and the farmer gets mad at the crows. But God has it so that everybody gets some," he said. So I realize that I don't own any idea, and once you put it out there, someone else (one way or another) is going to profit from it. I simply try to harvest my portion instead of procrastinating. So by the time others catch up to my idea, God has already moved me on to the next idea. You keep moving, learning, growing, and praising God.

I was still contracting work out to Delores and Tony of A&D Embroidery, with whom I became very close. I was

---

[2] http://attic.areavoices.com/2011/11/taystee-bakery-closes-in-duluths-west-end-1987/

working out of their business place and my basement. I also contracted silk screening jobs out to Reggie at B&B Factory, who was also very helpful to me. Once he told me, "Robert you need to get your own equipment." "No," I said. I was very happy bringing my business to him and making the few dollars I made off each job. But he told me how he started out and that there was nothing like having a creative idea in the middle of the night and being able to go into your shop, not depending on someone else to make it happen. I tell these stories because people always say that everybody is out for themselves. He didn't have to tell me this; he was making good money off of my business. But he encouraged me to step out, expand my wings, and to fly.

LEASING A SHOP: IT'S GOD WHO DIRECTS THE FLOW OF TRAFFIC

At my wife, Jo Ann's, suggestion, I leased a building on Grand River over a flower shop owned by a sister, Barbara Turner, at the church in 2000. It was right next to a Baskin-Robbins Ice Cream Parlor. I could not believe it. "Lord! I have my own business place!" And it was not far from home. My wife and I moved all my equipment and clothing supplies into our new establishment. Jo Ann sent out invitations for an open house for family, friends, and customers. It was a big day.

It was like I had my mind around any creative idea where I thought I could make an honest dollar; I would figure out how to develop it. I was still working full-time at AT&T with great work reviews and bonuses. God was so good to me, and He didn't allow me to fall. I was still contracting business out to A&D who would often tease me about how they taught me and that I had now learned more about the business and that they now called on me for advisement. God put me around people who were unselfish. I was and I'm still determined to learn from that, and with God's help I will demonstrate the same.

I remember once being very angry at the managers at AT&T. First, let me remind you that I was very happy with my position, and I was earning a really good salary. I had not even considered a promotion. It was not even on my radar. But my current manager at that time thought I should be in line for a promotion and that it was overdue. She submitted my name for a promotion, but her manager rejected it. She submitted my name a second time for promotion. Once again he declined the request and told her something to the effect of not submitting my name again and asked her if this was a black thing.

Reluctantly, she told me what had happened and said she didn't understand, with all the awards and accomplishments, why my name had never been submitted. She took another position at AT&T.

Well, of course, I got angry with thoughts of black versus white. In my mind, I rambled on and on. I was having a party in myself about what they were doing to me and how wrong it was. But the Holy Spirit began to talk to me and calm me down. He said, "You are not a dog that is jumping up at a bone." He asked me, "Why are you worried about what they did or didn't do?" He reminded me how it was that He opened the door against the odds and got me the job at AT&T, and it was He that had me there working like I wanted to ~ when I wanted to ~ how I wanted to, and getting paid top salary with bonuses. And at the same time using AT&T resources to build your business, and you're worried about a bone?

The Holy Spirit was so right. I thank God for God. I know that may not make sense to some, but I thank Him. AT&T was trying to save money and decided that all managers should work from home (smile). They paid for our internet, cellphones, and equipment. I could roll out of bed in my pajamas and say, "This is Bob Anderson, AT&T," or if the other phone rang, "Images of My People Productions, this is Robert." I could be at my shop on Grand River filling a customer order and at the same-time on the computer logged into any AT&T ACUS equipment that I managed around the states resolving most issues. AT&T could keep the bone.

BUILDING A SHOP BEHIND MY RESIDENCE:

Since most of my business was by word of mouth, I was never really in the shop except in the evenings and on weekends. I decided that it was not cost effective leasing the space, so I was going to buy a building. In my mind, I could see a building with a big business sign out in front extending over the door. My wife, who was very supportive, and I began looking for a suitable building that met all needs, location, etc. This building on Schoolcraft caught our eye. It wasn't too big; it was only two blocks away from where we lived. We proceeded to purchase. We got all the way to the day of signing and the deal fell apart. This was due to a family squabble among the sellers, which could have tied up our monies in court, if I had signed. I had taken out a loan and was reasonably upset. But God knew better. I was now looking for another building and prepared to spend money for any necessary modifications to make the building ready. My wife's cousin's husband, Kevin, asked me why was I so dead set on purchasing a building. I gave him all my reasons and that I needed to have a place where people could see my sign showing what I do. "But you are never there, and your business is by word of mouth." he argued with me. "Why don't you just have your garage torn down, and build your shop behind your home?" he asked. Finally, I heard what he was saying, and that turned out to be one of the best business decisions I made.

We contracted with Kevin and his business partner for the job. I now have a two-car garage (with shelving space), an adjacent room for work and display (with its own entry), a studio loft upstairs for photography (with a skylight window), and a furnace room with space for storage. All walls are finished and the building/garage has heat and air conditioning.

When the Pistons were in the Eastern Championship in 2004-2005 a business opportunity struck again. While others were sleeping, I was up all night in my shop burning Photo Dog Tags of key Piston players. I hit the streets, Seven Mile W. and Six Mile W, when people were getting off work. I was at the red light with dog tags of their favorite player dangling from chains. When they won the NBA Playoffs, I created other championship designs. Everybody wanted memorabilia. I sold out quickly at the Parades in downtown Detroit. Nobody had these but me, and I cashed in.

At Christmas, I came up with an incentive idea where others could share in my profits. For example: God had long ago shown me that every one of my customers were doors to others customers who could not get to me or that I would never meet. The key was getting to them. Chances were that if my current customer liked an item that I had made, someone who saw it would want it also. Especially those who worked in offices and had desks. Hence the SnowGlobe: the expense of the globe was $2.00 each, and sell for $20.00 each. The customer provides a photo you scan it, cut it to size, and insert it into the pretty snow globe. Let's say the work was $3.00, plus the expense $2.00 which was a total of $5.00 expense and $15.00 profit. People loved them with their babies, grandbabies, grandma, grandpa, dog, or cat. They would pick it up and shake it watching the snow fall. They were beautiful.

My mother's friend, Barbara McCoy, purchased one and loved it. She worked at a USPS facility and had a desk. I told her that all she needed to do if people wanted one was to collect the photos and the money. Now Barbara was not thinking about the money, but was doing it to help me. She called and said that she had twenty photo SnowGlobe orders. I picked the orders up and the money after she got off work, And I delivered the products the next day before she went to work and gave her $100.00 dollars (her incentive). Twenty photos times $5.00 equaled $100.00. When she saw how easy that was, I had created a monster. I hated when she retired. My point is that ideas are all around us, and you can't close your fist and not share the profits and/or blessings. It does not matter how beautiful the SnowGlobe looked; if no one ever saw it, no one would ever purchase it. Many times, God blesses us through others. Many people help us because they love God. Nobody has to do anything for you. Call it incentive or appreciation; either way we should not have a problem bestowing it.

No one can tell me that God does not have a sense of humor. I, who used to be a criminal mind, dope addict, and police hater who despised the police, that had run-ins with the police, and had many mugshots taken by the police, was now legally doing business with the police. My wife's cousin, who I won't name due to her current position as related to the law, was very supportive of me. I truly can't thank God enough for her and the part she played in my life story. She knew my past, she saw how God was changing my life, and she never stood off from me because of her position as Deputy Chief in the Detroit Police Department. This woman had me doing photography projects for the police department. She introduced me and my work to so many officers for whom I did photo work and made items. I even did work for Chief Bully. Sometimes I had to pinch myself, because even I could not believe this was actually happening. No one in my past life would had ever believed that this was possible. One day, there were so many ranking police officers in my shop behind my home, I know the neighbors probably thought I was being raided. But I was doing a group photograph. Every time I look at their various pictures on the wall, it is a reminder, and I thank God for where He has brought me.

Once I even remember attending a church assembly in the south, can't remember state because Spiritual Israel had churches in various states (often near a railroad, could never figure that out). I had never been there before and got lost. I could not find the church. A police cruiser was passing, so I flagged it down. I politely asked the officer if he could tell me how to get to the address that I had. He was a southern Caucasian officer, but he was very kind. In his southern voice he asked if I was looking for that Spiritual Israel Church & Its Army? I replied I was, and he said to follow him. Now this was really too much for me to handle. If the boys from back in my past could see me now! Here I was getting a police escort to CHURCH.

GOD GETS THE GLORY:

God showed me that He could clean me up, give me skills, teach me how to walk upright according to His Word, give me a stable home and marriage, enable me to start my own business, and to retire from AT&T. I am happy and my heart is glad, but now He is showing me that it never really was about me.

The skills I learned are being used for the church to help the ministry. Here I find so much joy. I heard when others said, "Only the things you do for Christ will last," (**1 Thessalonians 5:12-28**). What He did in, on, and through me was so He could get the glory. Somebody needs to know that there is life after death (sin) for those who would turn to Jesus Christ. There is hope for those who have lived a scarred life, and that they too can be washed in the blood of Christ if they just believe. I am not saying that I am an expert on Jesus Christ because of the life I lived and the things I did. But I am proof that He does love sinners (**John 3:16-21**) too and would have every man to be saved (**1 Timothy 2:4**). He is teaching me the truth of His Words that I might reach others and turn them toward Him which is our salvation. He is molding me in my marriage that I may walk upright before others in that which He ordained. He has made me a living example of what the Lord can do with a filthy rag. I have a new desire that means real success, that when I stand before Him, to hear my Lord say come in My good and faithful servant in whom I'm well pleased. I am not working to be saved (***Ephesians 2: 8-9***), but because I'm saved (***Romans 12: 1-2***).

CHAPTER SEVEN
QUESTION EVERYBODY

Question everything and everybody. Most people start the day with "Mirror Makeup" (*how they want others to perceive them*). I didn't know enough not to be satisfied until I had a sound answer. Most of the time I was looking for answers in all the wrong places. Leaning to my own understanding, I took things and people at face value, and so many times it was like stepping out on quicksand. The illusion was not that I sank quickly, but in reality, again and again. I invested my heart, soul, mind, body, and time in my own false image that I presented to people and borrowed from other people's *Mirror Makeups*. Somewhere along the way I got lost from Him that is the way, the truth, and the life (John 14:6). And I blamed everyone but myself for my spiral downwards below basement level.

REFLECTING ON MY YOUTH

Before coming to the west-side as a youth, I loved going to church. We lived on the east-side of Detroit, McDougall and Macomb, near what was then called black-bottom. I was respectful in our neighborhood and liked by many of the older people. I would work for them, and they taught me to cut lawns and plant flowers and to do things with my hands. Mrs. Adams was my favorite, she called me "my boy." At Christmas, she would give me gifts. There was another man that I would help with his lawn, and he fixed up a red wagon and gave it to me. I would use it to haul people's groceries for them at Laura Bros. Market. Another man in the neighborhood gave me a bicycle. My parents could not afford these things. From what I remember, my mother was the bread winner in the house, and my dad, Cleveland, would wash cars, when he could, at the gas station where he would be most of the time. Other men also hung out there and played the numbers.

Sometimes I would walk to the station and the music would be playing on the radio. My dad would have me dance, and I would do the splits and jump back up. The guys would edge me on clapping, and he would look at me so proud and say, "That is my son."

MOTHERS MAY NOT BE GREENER ON THE OTHER SIDE:

Mamma worked and daddy took care of the house and the cooking. I would earn pocket money helping on milk trucks delivering milk. As a kid growing up, I remember always hustling to make some change. Shoveling the snow, raking leaves, you name it. Here in this neighborhood I was at home, confident, and knew my place. But when my father left and we moved, I could never seem to adjust to the change. I didn't know the people in the neighborhood. I tried, but it was as if I was lost and trying to find myself or who I was. I was trying to identify myself.

There was a Presbyterian Church, on Clinton and Joseph Campau Street, around the corner from where we lived. The church was open almost every day and had activities and youth Bible classes. I loved going there. There was one minister, Reverend Glenn, that I remember who took time with me. He even took his belt to me one time, but I didn't care, because he always tried to help me. My parents were Baptist, and my mother attended a church where the well-known pastor killed his wife. The incident, unknown to him, was recorded on a tape recorder. My mother took this real hard, and sadly she left that church because he was out on bail and the members allowed him to sit in the pulpit which split the church. She later joined People Missionary Baptist Church, on Arndt and McDougall, where she served until her death in 2012.

When I told her that I wanted to join St. John Presbyterian Church and to be baptized there, it was out of the question. She stopped me from going there, and I had to attend People Missionary Baptist Church, where I was later baptized in 1956.

My mother moved the family to a place she rented on Warren and McDougall, near the church. It was here that I started getting into trouble in school and having a short attention span for what was being taught. The pastor, Reverend Charles Nicks, talked with me, and he even visited me at Juvenile Detention, but I just couldn't grasp what was being said to me. With no man in the house, I began to resent babysitting my sisters as my mother worked. I didn't understand that she was trying hard on her own to work and hold the family together. She laid down the law hard, and I rebelled. I started to run with boys that were older than I. So trying to keep me out of trouble, she sent me to stay with my grandmother, Mary Brown, for the summer on the west-side of Detroit. She could not work and worry about what I was doing. The problem was that my grandmother lived on Seward near 12th Street, where I was drawn into darkness portraying itself as light. For me, there was no going back.

Mabel was like my street mother. She was married to Fred Morris, my street father. I remember that she had gotten me a job with some of her relatives delivering the Michigan Chronicle's newspapers and Jet magazines to stores. It didn't pay much; so on Mother's Day, I took the little money I had and purchased identical towel sets (same price) for her and my real mother. But Mabel gave them back and told me something to the effect that it was cheap. I was crushed. My real mother accepted the gift with a smile and a hug, but I couldn't stay long because she had these church songs playing. I still did not realize the lesson that you only have one mother, that she did not abort me, and she had not turned her back on me. It pains me today to talk of my foolishness, my disobedience, my youthful arrogance, along with all the hurt and pain I caused my mother. But I speak on it now in hopes that it just may help somebody else. The grass was not, and is not greener on the other side. My mother loved Jesus, the Church, her children, and living upright. She loved all that I ran away from thinking and believing that there was something or someone better for me on the other side – in the streets.

NOT EVERYONE IS A FATHER FIGURE:

My father, Cleveland Anderson, had adopted me (at the age of three) as his son when he and my mother were married, and my last name was changed to Anderson. I never knew or can recall a good relationship with my biological father, Robert Talton, I knew. I longed for that relationship.

I loved both of my grandmothers, and they loved me. But the relationship with Grandma Talton and my aunts was strained. When I was younger, my mother would allow me to spend the night at my grandparents' house, but they would drill me asking, "Who is your father?" I would reply that Cleveland Anderson was my father. They would say, "NO, Robert Talton is your father." It was confusing, so my mother stopped me from spending the night there. When I got a little older, I would walk to Grandma Talton's house, and I was always received with open arms. After I started running away and got involved in the streets, I fell further away from my father's side of the family, especially after the drugs. Some things just can't be repaired and time brings about so many changes, including death.

Robert was married to a lady named Mary; she had one son, Ping, from a previous marriage. The rest of the children born of their marriage were my siblings. I also had another sister, Sharon, born to his first marriage. After his death, I found out that I had other siblings as well. As the song says, "Pop Was A Rolling Stone." My mother later told me that three women (including her) were pregnant with his child at the same time, and at first he denied that I was his, but Grandma Talton later resolved that I was his (I resembled her). The few times I spent the night at my father's home, it was never the one-on-one time with him that I longed for. However, Mary was very kind to me and she made me feel welcome. Looking back, it seemed that I had more of a relationship with her than I did with my own father. I was jealous of my father's relationship with Ping. I don't ever remember Robert being there for me, and until I got involved in the church, years later, I hated him for it. The only time I ever remember Robert coming to see me, was when I was an adult, and was on life support due to a gunshot wound in the back. I remember opening my eyes once and saw him there, that was it.

Even so, Cleveland was my daddy, and it was his love that I grew to know and love; he was my father. My mother was working at Reliable Linen Laundry, and during this time, my father, Cleveland, was out of work. They told me and my sisters that he was going to Seattle, Washington to get a job and that we would later move there. It would be years later when I finally understood that they had been actually separating.

I was like a bird that flew out of a cage when we moved to the west-side of Detroit, off of 12th Street. I had begun running away from home about the age of fifteen (1962-1963). I remember being on 12th Street when it was reported that President John F. Kennedy was assassinated, I liked hanging around people that were older than I, and much of what I learned was from a man named Little Fred. He was like a father figure to me (at least in my mind). He had several after-hour joints on the west side of Detroit. Everybody talked about Fred Morris, and I wanted to be like him. I even changed my name to Bobby Morris and told everybody he was my father. I began to sell corn liquor and beer for him in the after-hour joint, learning the ins and outs and how to cut craps for the house running dice and/or card games. I remember setting up Black Label beer containers to make a bar across the kitchen door entrance. I would use the kitchen wall to keep track of what I sold and to add/subtract figures for making change, etc. I would be up all night until I just couldn't keep my eyes open. I was foolishly where I thought I wanted to be (grown). The funny thing is I don't remember getting paid, I was just glad to be there, and, good or bad, I was learning the streets.

I wanted to be accepted. In my mind, it was father and son. If you had a problem with Fred, you had a problem with me. Fred drank and needless to say, there were a lot of problems. One time he even pulled his knife on me because Mabel, his wife, had brought me a pair of shoes for Easter. I left crying but was right back there in a few days, like nothing ever happened. Truth is, I needed and wanted my daddy. I had to learn the hard way, that everybody is not a father figure.

STREETS LOVE CHILDREN WHO WANT TO BE GROWN:

Sometimes, in the after-hour joint during the winter nights on 12th and Seward, it got so cold I had to sleep with newspaper over me to keep warm. I didn't have a bed, but I would put two or three chairs together. The crazy thing about this was that my loving mother and a warm bed were only a few blocks away at 12th and Philadelphia, but I was street blind.

Sometimes the police would raid the place and catch me trying to escape. But it was not Fred who showed up, but my mother who had to take off from her job to come and see about me in juvenile. I'd promise I was going to do better, but no sooner than the detention doors swung open, I was right-back on 12th Street.

Believe it or not, I even tried going back to school at Washington Trade School while living in the after-hour joint. I remember that some of the guys (not me) in the classroom were throwing paper spit-balls and the instructor was going to paddle all the boys in the class (as the teachers were allowed to do back in those days). But not me, I was not having it! I foolishly told the principal that I was too adult for such things, I was taking care of myself, and was only there to get a trade. He applauded me wanting to get an education, but said the school system could not allow me to attend school there under those conditions. I could not be a kid and an adult, so back to the after-hour joint (school of life) I went.

In my new world on 12th Street, I was still trying to hold on to Jesus no matter how skewed my view. One Sunday I had a mind to go to church. I don't know why, because I hadn't been to church in a long time. Since I wasn't getting paid, I didn't have any money. I asked Fred, my street father, for some money to put in church, but he told me something to the effect that he wasn't going to give me any money to put in some preacher's pocket. It would be many years later before I ever even mentioned anything about a church to him again.

Snake was about ten years older than I. I was about seventeen or going on eighteen when I first met him in Fred's after-hour joint. Snake had it going on street-wise, and I wanted to be just like him. I wanted to be accepted. We became like brothers. If you had a problem with him, you had a problem with me. I remember once in he was in a gambling game, and he got in an argument with another guy. I wanted to prove myself so much that I took the gun out of his hand and would have used it. On another occasion, someone had disrespected his wife, and he called me because if you messed with him, you messed with me.

When the use of drugs became a dominant stronghold in and on my life (Snake didn't use drugs), the relationship became strained and lopsided. I remember calling him because I had gotten into some trouble, and some guys were gunning for me. I called Snake, but he told me that he was in bed with his wife and couldn't come. This was my brother? I could not believe what I was hearing. How many times had I come when he called, day or night? I was so hurt and felt brotherly abandonment. I thought to myself over and over, "How could he not be there for me as I was for him?" I wanted to get even and back at him, even hurt him, but I still cared about him, and unknown to me God wouldn't allow me to do the things that came to mind. It was that same Snake, Nathaniel Cook, who years later told me about God in a dope house. It was he that that gave me a tie and brought me to The Spiritual Israel Church & Its Army. The greatest thing, as a brother, that he could ever do was to turn me back towards God, and for that I will always be thankful to him.

In 1966 I turned eighteen, and shortly afterwards, Uncle Sam sent a letter of induction to my mother's house. Streetwise, I thought I had it going on. I was now in true hustler mode, but as not to give false glory to the streets, I'll minimize the details. You could not tell me anything. I was determined that I was too cool for that army stuff. So once again thinking I was outsmarting everyone else, I outsmarted myself. After all, I was not going to Viet Nam to die for a country that didn't care about me.

I asked some of the older street associates how I could get around or out of being drafted. Somebody suggested that I could pretend to be gay with some ideas of what to do. Nope, that was a no-no. In my mind that was not even an option. Somebody else, I don't even remember who it was, said, "They reject dope fiends."

Before this time, we thought we were better than junkies. No matter what you did, at least you were not a junkie shooting up with needles and syringes. I theorized all I needed to do was get tracks all up and down my arms for a good showing. I wasn't going to shoot the heroin like dope fiends do. I would do just enough so that when I went down there on my day, they'd find it in my system. After that, I'd go back to normal. I don't recall anyone saying that it was a bad idea. It worked! On my day to report, I remember going down there scratching and nodding like the junkies do. I had it down to a "t." They examined me, took urine samples, and rejected me. As I was leaving, I recall looking over into a room at the guys taking the oath, and I said to myself, "Them suckers." Little did I know and it would be many years (and tears) too late before I acknowledge that I was the real sucker. I had sold my soul to the devil and didn't know how to get it back.

It was not until about 1981 while attending service in The Spiritual Israel Church & Its Army, that I first heard that "every time I pointed my finger out at someone else that I have three fingers and a thumb pointing back at me." I had become so used to the broken record "if it had not been" for [him, her, this, or that]. More importantly, I learned to question myself in relation to God's Word. "If it had not been for the Lord who was on my side, where oh where would I be?" ***(Psalm 124:1-2)***.

LEARNING WHAT WAS HIDING IN MY HEART:

Many times, parents attempt to keep their children from other children that they perceive as the bad element. I remember, as a child, having a love for Jesus based on who I knew Him to be. Of course, I was too young to understand doctrine, but I knew what I was told, "Jesus loved me." Never was I asked how do I know that I love him. Growing up as a child, we had the humble Caucasian Jesus with blue eyes and long hair on our wall with a halo over His head staring at you. There was also the picture of Jesus at the Last Supper.

As a child, I can't remember my mother reading the Scripture with me or to me. Not to say that she didn't, I just don't remember it. But she did teach me to pray before I went to bed at night. ***"Now I lay me down to sleep, I pray the***

Lord my soul to keep. If I should die before I wake, I pray the Lord my soul to take."

But what did it mean? I was afraid of death, dead people, and the cemetery. I was afraid of the church radio programs that my mother would listen to on Sunday nights advertising Diggs Funeral Home Services in a low solemn and scary voice (to me). No one explained those things to me. When mom's lady friends lost a loved one who had died in the house, why did she volunteer me to stay at their house for them to be comforted? Who was going to comfort me when I was afraid?

My Grandma, Mary Brown, did not go to church. Grandma loved her Red Seal snuff, and back in the day a little lightening juice, or beer with a straw. Even though grandma didn't attend church, she had her Bible and loved her Jesus. I have the memory of her reading the Lord's Prayer to me from the Bible. I was her first grandchild. She loved me, and I loved her. She always made me feel that if I could make it to grandma's house, everything would be alright. When my mother was going to whip me, I'd run to grandma's house, and that would make my mother so angry. As a child, I drew a picture of Jesus with a halo and crosses all around Him. I may have been about 7 or 8 years old. But my Grandma hung that picture over her dresser. Whenever I would visit her and see the drawing, I would laugh inside myself because it was obvious that I could not draw, but it was a reminder to me of her love hanging on her wall. She never got rid of it, and it hung in her home until she passed away.

Not to say, that grandma spared the switches on my tail. Once she was doing cleaning in her home, where she lived was called Black Bottom. There was a house-store directly next door. As she cleaned, she had taken everything off the bed and the mattress was turned back. There in the middle of the bed was a shiny penny that was hypnotizing me. I went in and out of the door several times looking at that penny. Grandma just kept sweeping the floor as if she didn't see me. Finally, I built-up my nerve to pick up that shiny penny. Out the door I went to the store and bought a penny candy, a squirrel. As soon as I walked out of the store, grandma was waiting for me with a switch.

I was afraid of whippings, especially from my mother. But being afraid never seemed to stop me from doing wrong and getting into trouble. I must have been about 5 or 6 years old; my mother had told me to keep things out of my mouth. I had a set of jacks that children played with back in that day. That night in bed I had put a jack in my mouth and swallowed it. It was choking me. My mother was upset and hysterical crying, "Oh my baby," while trying to figure out what it was that was choking me. She asked me if it was a tooth? Nodding my head, I said un huh, (meaning yes) it was a tooth. She was renting a room at that time from Mr. & Mrs. Sherman. Mr. Sherman picked me up, turned me upside down, and hit me on the back. Out came the jack. When my mother saw that the tooth was actually a jack, she started hitting on me. This same woman who was just crying, "Oh my baby," was now threatening to kill me if I ever lied to her again. They had to pull her off of me.

Fear does not necessarily keep people from doing or thinking wrong, but true love will. My point is that no one taught me to lie and no one taught me to steal, and yet it was in me:

> "Behold, I was shapen in iniquity; and in sin did my mother conceive me." (**Psalm 51:5**).

> "The heart is deceitful above all things, and desperately wicked: who can know it?" (**Jeremiah 17:9**).

None of the other things I did as a child were taught to me, even though I drew pictures of Jesus and said I loved Him. Who could I blame it on and where were the bad elements? At this stage of my life, there were none. I was taken to church as a child and taught to sit at attention, and I was baptized at the age of eight. And as I grew and got into trouble, I would call on Jesus for that moment. I even wore a cross around my neck, and sometimes a cross earring in my ear. But I had no reality of Jesus Christ in my life. I'd gone through the phase of who needs **a white Jesus** and **the white man wrote the Bible**. When you want to escape from the Biblical Jesus, there is always someone ready and willing to give you a boat. But no matter how wicked I got or acted, the Jesus I didn't know would not let me be. Other than His love, I can't explain why He didn't give up on me, even though around others I had come to deny Him and had given up on Him. Why me, the chief of sinners? Without His blood covering me, I would be most miserable, engulfed in my sins. But instead it helped me to understand just how much I was in need of a Savior and that I needed saving from myself.

> "**If we confess our sins**, he is faithful and just to forgive us our sins, and to cleanse us from all unrighteousness"(**1 John 1:9**).

I needed a tangible relationship with Jesus Christ. It is this convicting relationship that keeps me from lying, stealing, committing adultery, or anything else. Not by saying I won't do this or that, but trusting in and submitting to Him, and the Word of God in order to keep me from doing this or that:

> "**Submit yourselves therefore to God**. Resist the devil, and he will flee from you. 8 **Draw nigh to God, and he will draw nigh to you**. Cleanse your hands, ye sinners; and purify your hearts, ye double minded." (**James 4:7-8**).

He is my ever ready help and strength. I no longer fight self with self, that is a losing battle. But He has given us of His Spirit (**John 14:23**).

MY DAUGHTER BORN IN THE CROOKEDNESS OF MY LIFE:

In 1972, my daughter was born, Alicia Dionne Anderson. At that time, I was not equipped mentally and spiritually to be a real father. Though I tried with everything that was in me, the deck was stacked against me: self, court, drugs, my-baby-mama, no job, and blame.

I was a drug dealer and Linda, her mom, was selling drugs for me in Herman Garden's apartments where she lived with her two children. We were having an affair even though I was still married to Bea at that time. In street life, fornication and adultery are words that do not exist. In fact, even the word hell, is never used in the Biblical sense. Hell was what you deal with in the streets.

Linda was making a sale and was shot in the back. This is when we found out that she was pregnant. I left Bea and moved in with Linda. I loved my daughter and gave her my last name, but I had nothing else to give her because I was lost and didn't even realize it.

Eventually Linda and I parted ways, but I still wanted to be in my daughter's life. But Linda by this time had another man, and the relationship was strained. I didn't know it then, but there is a reason that God has His people to marry one man and one wife. Anything outside of God's plan is full of trouble and consequences; I was about to find that out. Throughout my daughter's early life, it was as if I was a fly on the wall.

I had called to see my daughter, Dee-Dee (that was what we called her), but her mother would not allow it. I decided that I was going over to see her any way. When I got there, the man Linda was seeing opened the door, and I told him why I was there and walked in. Linda was arguing at me, but I noticed that my daughter was responding druggy and I picked her up. Angry, while Linda was trying to stop me, I said, "She is going to the hospital." We learned at the hospital that she had gotten hold of some of Linda's pills. Let's just say I wanted to kill somebody.

I didn't want my baby to go back into Linda's home. There was an investigation, and how soon I learned that it did not matter that I was the child's father. She was placed into foster care. She was later returned to Linda, but other problems kept coming up and my daughter would be in and out of foster care again and again. I attended the court proceedings, and it was like I was not even there. My mother and I would always form a good relationship at the homes where they would allow me to visit and even take Dee-Dee with me to spend time. But somehow Linda found out, and she complained to the social worker who put a stop to it. They were even unwilling to put her in my mother's care because Linda was vengeful. If she could not have her, she was not going to allow me to have my daughter or access to her.

I tried to even clean myself up and got married (2nd time). During this time, I was not praying, seeking God, or going to any church. I was trying to fight my own battle, hating Linda and complaining to anyone who would listen to me. I was doing part-time work and got a little apartment in the hope of getting custody. Linda was living at Big Mama's house, the other children's aunt. Most of the time they didn't know where Linda was and when they could not find her, the social worker would bring Dee-Dee to me. Then a couple of days later she would call for me to take her back to Big Mama's house. But Linda was not there, I complained. When I refused, the social worker would threaten to have a warrant issued for my arrest. My mother and aunt, in an effort to protect me, would pick my daughter up and drop her off at Big Mama's house. I wanted to tell the social worker "to hell with it," and don't call me anymore when you can't find Linda. But I loved my daughter, and I just could not say it.

Once the court gave me temporary custody, but every time we would go to court it was always another judge. One judge had the nerve to ask me who I was paying support to while I had custody of the child. He didn't even know it. The court system was a joke, but I was a part of it and was bitter and hateful. I loved my daughter, but it was as if no one cared but my daughter. She loved me and would cling to me only to be snatched out of my arms again and again.

The last straw was the day that Linda set me up. She knew my temper, and I walked right into the trap. I had custody of my daughter and was at home in bed with my wife, Deborah. Linda called my apartment about 5:00 a.m. or 6:00 a.m. in the morning and demanded that I put my daughter on the phone. I said that she was asleep and suggested she call back at a more appropriate hour. The conversation didn't go very well. She said she was coming over and that I better have her ready. A long story made short; she and her sister came pushing their way into my apartment, and we got into a battle. I had called the police; when they arrived, she was out of control. I showed the officers my custody papers and told them what had happened. Her explicit language with the officers and battery caused them to take her to jail. The officers informed me that I should go to the station if I wanted to file charges.

The social worker came and picked my daughter up that same day. It didn't matter that the incident was not of my making. I walked into it! The social worker gave me some spiel about trying to be fair and letting the court decide. Well, the court decided, it was another judge, they gave Linda custody, and nothing was said of me. I was done and a broken man. I walked out of the court telling them all what they could do for me (I was not saved). I didn't care if they would have locked me up. I felt that there was nothing else they could do to me; they had stripped me of the one I loved most, my daughter. It would be over ten years before I saw my daughter again. Linda got married and changed my daughter's last name to her maiden name and hid her from me. Meanwhile I retreated into drugs and feeling sorry for myself. I used to say "If I saw a Mack Truck about to run over her that I would look the other way. I could care less." I hated Linda with a passion.

Years later after I joined The Spiritual Israel Church & Its Army, thoughts of Linda were far behind me. I no longer gave her thought even though I didn't know where my daughter was. One day the congregation was singing a song about love, and loving everybody. I was really into the song and singing along, clapping my hands, and moving my feet, while thinking that I loved everybody. Then the Holy Spirit spoke and asked me the question, "What about Linda?" My mouth fell open, and I stopped in my tracks. I had forgot about Linda and the awful things I had said. I had to pray and ask God's forgiveness and to "create in me a clean heart and renew the right spirit with in me" (**Psalm 51:10**). "Who can understand his errors? cleanse thou me from secret faults" (**Psalm 19:12).** God will show you yourself. I was learning that there is more to loving God than just singing about love.

Regardless of what she did or didn't do – was I any better? Keep in mind my life was not right, so I can't blame Linda without looking at myself. When I look back through those pages, I now see myself also. What did I bring to the table in a father role? A child can't eat love. What about my lifestyle? I didn't even know who I was or would ever be, and I was not doing anything to change my situation. The main thing was that I didn't know God in order to bring her to Him. But it had been easier to see Linda rather than looking at myself.

The sad thing is that you can't fix broken children, and you can't undo time. I love my daughter, and I believe she loves me. But that bond that we used to have, I could never seem to mend. So many things occurred in that time span, and there is a gap that only God can fill.

I often give the example of drug addict parents with a child. The parents are busy fulfilling their drug needs, while the child's needs are unmet. The child may be bounced around from here to there due to the adverse conditions of the scenario. The child begins to depend on self, looking to friends for love, relationships, and advice. This goes on for years. Then one day the parents wake-up from the nightmare and decide that they want to clean themselves up and turn their life around. The parents find God and start going to church. But they don't understand what in the world is wrong with their child; why are they acting like they do? They had better straighten up and fly right.

    The child does not turn on and off like a switch. While you were broken, and trying to get yourself together, TIME DOES NOT STAND STILL with your child in a bubble. What we do affects those connected to us. You were not the only one that was broken by your choices. The decisions you made causes your child to be broken also. The family needs healing that only God can provide. And for those who have not gone down this road yet, remember God knows best, and when we ignore His instructions, there are consequences for our choices. God has had mercy on me, but there are still consequences to the choices that I made. I pray this serves as a warning to others. Touch a hot stove, and you will get burned. You will heal, but the scar is the consequence.

CHAPTER EIGHT
GOD KNOWS - STORY OF THE NAILS

When I joined The Spiritual Israel Church & Its Army, Temple #8, in 1980-81, I was so zealous. I loved working in the church. They later trusted me with a set of keys to the church; me the chief of sinners. I would come and clean up the building on Saturday nights. I would stop and pick something up to eat, and if I got tired I would lay out on one of the pews. As time progressed, I was elevated from a brother to a Deacon and would work with the Jr. Deacons. I would pick them up to help maintain the church. Some of us Deacons would sing Church songs in between working, and I loved those days. I remember us down on our knees tiling the basement of the church where the dining hall and kitchen where. It was a project that I started, but many of the Deacons assisted me in the project. I had never taken on anything like this, and when it was completed, I was so excited about what we had done.

I learned Israel Doctrine and was elevated to the minister's board. The Assistant Pastor passed, and many of the women in the church were talking about who they thought should be the new Assistant Pastor. All I could hear them talking about was my spiritual brother, Edward Mack, who was also a minister; how he had done this in the church and how he had done that in the church. I must admit it got to me, "What about what I had done," I thought to myself.

But then the Holy Spirit showed me this: Look at the walls and how perfect they are painted; Look at the pretty blinds and curtains on the windows; Look at the trimming, the finishing's, and the ledges where the beautiful flower pots sit. And yet take away the **nails** that nobody talks about and all these pretty things will come tumbling down. Nobody sees and talks about how beautiful and strong the nails are that hold all these things together. But God knows where every single nail is in the church and its function. He knows!

After this, I got me a bunch of nails and put a rubber band around them. I carried this around with me as a reminder not to worry about what people say and to be happy with what God sees. Reverend Edward Mack was the right person for the job. He later was elevated to Elder and became pastor after Mother Rose passed. He elevated me to an Elder and I became his Assistant Pastor. As strange as it may be, it was Elder Edward Lee Mack that first said something is wrong in Israel, and that Jesus Christ needed to be preached. Because of his words, God began to open my eyes. Elder Mack is still in The Spiritual Israel Church & Its Army and believes he can change the doctrine. I don't.

SOMETIMES WALKING AWAY IS BEST

You could never have told me, Robert, one day you are going to walk away from The Spiritual Israel Church & Its Army. I would have called you a liar to the 10th degree. For me, everything good that had happened in my life was attributed to The Spiritual Israel Church & Its Army. The way that I had been taught was that there was no separating "The God of Israel" from "The Spiritual Israel Church & Its Army." You respected the leadership, and you didn't question it, at least not out loud. There were minor things that I had begun to challenge such as finances but nothing that would cause me to walk away. Elder Edward Mack, our pastor, was preaching this particular day, and said "that Jesus needed to be preached in Israel's doctrine and that you can't get to the Father without Him." To me this would be the day that *"Humpty Dumpty sat on a wall, Humpty Dumpty had a great fall; and all of the King's horses and all of the King's men couldn't put Humpty together again."* He had put into words everything I had been believing in my soul. If that was true, then I needed to leave and find a church where Jesus was being preached. In 2002 my wife and I walked away.

The remaining part of my story is less about me and more about the organization that God used to clean me up.

CHAPTER NINE
BELIEVE GOD IS ABLE ~ HEALING

The song[3] says, "I looked at my hands and they looked new and looked at my feet and they did too." Yes, God had healed my body from the many years of abuse. Even so, I knew there were consequences from the choices that I had made. For a person to leave The Spiritual Israel Church & Its Army meant they were no longer following the real God and had returned to the world (Christianity). I will explore this more later in the chapter that discusses Israel's doctrine. Thank God I didn't get sick or die. In the mind of Israel's members that would have been proof that I should never have left. Even though people do get sick and die in The Spiritual Israel Church & Its Army, when that happens they blame it all on sin. In other words, you sinned, that's why you got sick or died.

I joined Strictly Biblical Bible Teaching Ministry about 2007. As a new member, I was attending Strictly Biblical Bible Teaching Ministry when I got diagnosed with Hepatitis C and Prostate Cancer. I came home feeling low and didn't want to talk to anyone, not even my wife, who was at work at the time. I laid across the bed and pulled the cover over my head as if I could hide. I thought about what the people back in Israel would say, "See what happened to him?"

There was no Mother Rose as in the past for me to run to like I'd done so many times before. I felt alone. But the Holy Spirit began to talk to me and comfort me, saying, "How many times do I have to come to your rescue before you have faith in me? How many more Bible verses do you have to read? How many more people do you need to run to and ask

---

[3] Jones, George. *My Soul's Been Satisfied.* Country Church Time Album (1959).

them to pray for you before you start believing and having faith? I got you off drugs; I got you off alcohol; I cleaned you! It was me that got you a job at AT&T and held you there. It was me that gave you a stable home and a wife. It was me that opened doors for you that no man could close. I've done this and I've done that; now you get up and go into the bathroom and wash your face and lift up your head."

I was obedient to the Holy Spirit, and I washed my face and cheered up preparing for the road ahead. I continuously reminded myself of all that He had done for me down through the years as I took my treatments day in and day out. I lost weight and was so weak that I could barely stand. But I held on to the Lord. Sometimes I wanted to go to Church but could make it no further than the foot of the bed. When I could make it to Church the Praise Team didn't have to tell me to lift my hands or stomp my feet praising God. They just didn't know that all week long I was too weak to do so, and I was happy to be in the House of the Lord. I was going to lift my hands because I didn't know what I'd be able to do tomorrow.

I didn't talk on the phone much, not because I was ashamed, but most of the time I was too weak. And I didn't want to replay my illness; and I was not looking for pity. I just wanted to focus on God. It wasn't that I was too proud to ask for prayer, but I wanted "the one-on-one" with God. I wanted to take God at His Word. I wanted to do things not because Mother Rose said so, the pastor said so, or the Bible stories said so. But because the Holy Spirit said so. If He delivered me back then, He is the same God, and if it is His Will, He could deliver me again.

I learned to thank God for my wife, Jo Ann, and to appreciate her (I'm still learning). I knew she loved me, but when you can't do for yourself and you see how someone is attentive to your every need, you know they must love you. She watched me like a hawk. She had gotten a scare when I passed out and fell. All she could think about was how was she going to pick me up?

Well, God brought me through both. I am free and clear of Hepatitis C and Prostate Cancer. People can pray for you, but sooner or later, you are going to have to know Him for yourself. I won't take nothing for the relationship with Jesus Christ in my life. And I still pray, "Lord increase my faith."

CHAPTER TEN
THE DOCTRINE OF ISRAEL IN RETROSPECT:

The doctrine of Israel in a nutshell: "***The World***" in Israel refers not only to the secular world, but includes any and all religious institutions and organizations that are not of The Spiritual Israel and Its Army. The church was established as an ecclesiastical organization in 1935. One man rules – The King of Israel. All members that performed any prayer or other type of activity in the church before the people must say, "**I Rise and Give Honor to The Holy Father, The King of Israel**." When I first joined the organization, Bishop Robert Haywood was the King of Israel, so we had to add his name when saying it, but saying his name was later dropped. This was done because it was preached that **in every generation God had a man to lead his people Israel**, based on *1 Kings 9:5*. And if you were not Israel, **you could not be saved** based on *Romans 11:26.* We were taught that we were not Christians, because **God formed Israel** (*Isaiah 43:1-6*) and that **God's name is Israel** so he called us Israel (*Isaiah 43:7*); And that **Israel is our Father** (*Genesis 49:2*). Every preacher basically preached the same message pointing to Scriptures with Israel in them, and the readers would read them out loud.

WHY DO PEOPLE GRAVITATE TOWARDS FALSE TEACHING?

I believe that The Spiritual Israel Church & Its Army gave my life stability without understanding that this stability was built on a false foundation and the premise of salvation. This organization addressed my need for identity and worth. In retrospect that which was good for me (or to me), could have been the damnation of me. Broken people for various reasons are susceptible to false doctrines. Many could not see the truth if it was staring them in the face because of emotions, trauma, bad experiences, greed, desires, identity crisis, weaknesses, or self-perceived false notions about God and self. The problem was not that we didn't want God, but that we unknowingly wanted Him according to our specifications, which is unbiblical. We wanted a mail order God. Don't take my word for it, step outside of the box and listen to what people are actually saying about God compared to what the Bible, His record, actually teaches us about Him. If you are honest with yourself, perhaps it may have happened to you.

In my case I was lost with the Bible in my hands. It is only through redemption and the grace of God that I am able to report what I have experienced, learned, seen, and heard. Some will say, perhaps with arrogance, that would (or could) never happen to me. It is my prayer that it doesn't happen to you or anyone you know. But it doesn't take much to see that false teachings are spreading into the denominational and non-denominational churches of today at what should be an alarming rate. The gospel songs are changing and becoming secular and false teachers are allowed into the pulpits of what were known as sound doctrinal Churches. It seems I am running away (escaping) from the cults and the false doctrine that I was entrapped in for over thirty years only to find that many churches (not all) are embracing false doctrine in one form or another.

While I am not implying that everybody is the same, the craft of a con man (false teacher) is to appear to address a need or a want while taking you along for the journey. False doctrines could not flourish if they were not giving the illusion of fulfilling a need in people. What I have learned through talking to others and studying cults and false doctrines is that each lie is packaged with you in mind. You, the broken person, simply stepped up to the counter. It is difficult to sell people something they don't want or are not looking for. The truth of the matter is this, there is a market for false doctrine and the suppliers are many.

For example:

- If you have a problem with the blue-eyed, white Jesus hanging on your great-grandma and your mama's walls, who looks like the system and society that has its feet on your neck? No problem. Let me teach you about the black Jesus that the white man didn't want you to know about. They stole your identity, but God sent me to get you.

- You tired of being broke? The tail and not the head? It is because you are a god, but the problem was you didn't know it. God sent me to wake you up to who you really are.

- You tired of being sick? Let me prophesy over your life. Let me speak life into your body and teach you that you have power in your words, and you can call things that are not as though they were.

- Did you know that death is an illusion? There is no heaven or hell. Let me teach you how to be one with the universe.

- All the other religions are wrong, and God and Jesus gave me a revelation to call His people out of bondage. If you want to be saved, follow me.

- The Bible is a poisoned book, and Christianity is the white man's religion. The Koran is corrupt, but Allah sent me to fetch and teach his people.

These are a few examples, and the list, goes on and on. It does not matter the name of the cult or false doctrinal organization whether it be the Nation of Islam, the New Nation of Islam, World Islam, the Mormons, The Jehovah Witnesses, The Word of Faith Movement, The Black Hebrew Israelites to name just a few. They all share the same element (ingredient) "FALSE." While I was studying apologetics under

Pastor Emery Moss Jr., I learned that he had never heard of "The Spiritual Israel Church & Its Army." But as he taught and exposed the doctrines of other false groups and cults, I found that I could identify with many of their various teachings in one form or another because many of those same things were taught in "The Spiritual Israel Church & Its Army" even though it was taught for the people to not be like the world (other religions). A lie will always be a lie no matter how it is packaged and regardless of the pretty colored bow you tie around the box; be it blue, red, gold, purple, or multicolor. There is still a lie in the box.

I came into Israel (the church) just as I was and knew nothing about the church doctrine and even less as it was related to the doctrine of Christ. What I did know was that I didn't know about Jesus Christ and His works, Christology. It would be almost thirty years before I ever got my hands on the documents that entailed the doctrinal statements of Israel. Even so truthfully, and with fear, I say that I don't think it would have made that much difference to me at that low stage of my life. Today I am shocked at my ignorance and bewildered that even so God used this organization to rescue me. To explain it would be to attempt to explain God. And that my friend I just can't do. What I do know is that God can and does work despite the fallibility of any organization or of us; my life and this book are proof of that. But this can never be a justification for joining a cult or false organization; we should never stay under cultic teachings or false doctrines when they have been exposed for what they are. Too many people are lost and have died in them.

When I did begin to question the teachings, my questions were often met with hostility. Many of us late comers had never read the original by-laws and rule books (known as the blue book, "The Rule," followed by yellow, "The Bylaw and Oracles"). The leaders that still had them would never let them out of their possession or let you look at it. But they never had issue with telling you what you were doing contrary to them. When I joined Israel under Bishop Robert Haywood, I obtained a newer updated version. However, I now know it does not have all the original doctrinal statements as the original. Those doctrinal statements may not exist in the new by-laws book, but they are still being taught, practiced, and enforced orally. The leadership that had the old by-laws would tell us to stick to the doctrine of Israel, but no one would ever answer my question: Is the doctrine of Israel the doctrine of Christ?

ACCORDING TO THE DOCTRINE OF ISRAEL:

The Creed states:

- We Believe that we are God's only People.
- We Believe that God chose us in Him before the foundation of the world.
- We Believe therefore our Spiritual name is Israel.
- We Believe that the Lord God of Israel **only speaks to one man** in a generation and **that man is the God-Head** and **mediator** for us.
- We believe that the nationality of the so-called Negros is Ethiopian; however we also believe that regardless to a person's race or nationality if they are willing to follow the way of Israel, they too can become Israelites.
- We believe that the Kingdom of God is peace, joy, and happiness and dwells in the hearts of men and women.
- We Believe that to serve God we must love and serve one another.
- We Believe in abiding by the law of the land. Our teaching does not approve of disobedience to any law.

- Finally, **We emphatically believe** that if we live true to the Lord God of Israel and keep His commandments, that He will save us in these bodies eternally.

No one passes out their creed to you when you join their church (or organization), but in my case, and I am sure others, I would not have known what to look for. I would never have noticed in my search for identity that Jesus Christ was missing from these seemingly fine words. Even so, it is only now after God drew me out and much study under the sound doctrine of Jesus Christ that I am able to expose the error that this unbiblical doctrine promotes. I expose it to save those in Israel, other cults, or false religions who believe they are saved under these and similar teachings which teach contrary to the doctrine of Christ, even though they may use a multitude of Scriptures (out of context) to support their Creed. My desire is to point people to Jesus Christ who is the true salvation to those who receive Him, according to Scripture.

You can be zealous about God and Jesus Christ, but being zealous does not equate to having knowledge of those that you are zealous about. It is my belief that the reason most people join Christian cults or false religions, after Christianity, is because they were not learned in sound Biblical doctrine. They became easy prey to wolves in sheep's clothing or to those that don't know that they themselves are Biblically blind. These seek to lead through either false interpretations of Scripture or the teachings of men passed off as the inspiration of some God that falls outside of Biblical revelation. Like thieves or magicians with "sleight of hand tricks" these use "sleight of words" to draw you unto a god of their imagination. In retrospect, it was not that the Bible was wrong, but we were taught to read it through the eyes of the leadership chosen by God, the so-called chosen Man-of-God.

The Doctrine of Israel in Retrospect

Now remember when I came to The Spiritual Israel Church & Its Army, I was broken, hopeless, and a sponge. I knew nothing about:

- reading in context, eisegesis, exegesis
- hermeneutics, apologetics, replacement theology, hamartiology
- historical revisionism, church history, soteriology, Christology
- What the Bible teaches about another Jesus (which is not another) (2 Corinthians 11:4)
- What the Bible teaches about another gospel (Galatians 1:6)

Please see the glossary for definitions of these words.

Don't think that I am referring to these terms for the sake of showing what I have learned. These are theological terms related to studies, practices (do's and don'ts), and doctrine that most sound Christians are Biblically aware of even though they are not familiar with the actual terms themselves. The problem is that I was not aware and neither were the people who were teaching me. Hence, heresies and false religions. Contrary to popular belief everyone with a Bible is not called by God. He wants us to understand His Word. But reading is one thing, studying is another, and comprehension brings what we have read and studied together in understanding. I am reminded of the Ethiopian eunuch:

> **Acts 8: 30** 31 – And Philip ran thither to him, and **heard him read the prophet Esaias**, and said, **Understandest thou what thou readest?** And **he said, How can I, except some man should guide me?** And he desired Philip that he would come up and sit with him.

The "**some man**" today should have applied himself under much prayer to study and know God's Word, before they attempt to teach others. These are not just any men and women, but those who have given themselves wholly to the study of God's Word. The problem today is that:

- Anyone can establish a church or non-biblical religion.
- There is no accountability related to doctrine (free for all).
- People don't question what is passed off as sound doctrine.
- Most say that God called them, and they don't need any one to teach them.
- People have itching ears, and to many of them doctrine doesn't matter.
- False churches will license anyone who will learn and defend their unbiblical doctrine.
- There is a market for false doctrine and it gives the illusion of meeting people's needs.
- Many have no clue what sound doctrine (doctrine of Christ) is; they simply know that they are in need of something.
- People become complacent and happy where they are, and they're afraid to question authority.
- Even when the church doctrine becomes questionable, people feel a sense of belonging. They become loyal to the church (organization) in place of being loyal to God and His Word.

As for me, you never could have told me I would question or leave The Spiritual Israel Church & Its Army. I would have given my life for it, but God peeled that onion.

CHAPTER ELEVEN
THE ART OF TWISTING SCRIPTURES:

Note: [*Bullet points and bold text added by me to provide emphasis on the borrowed references.*]

We were taught that the Bible was not a book that you could just read straight through; not if you wanted to get an understanding. Jesus said these things were hid from the wise and prudent (Matthew 11:25). The minister would preach with smooth rhythmic words, metaphorically and leading, explaining for his rationale of hopscotching all over Scriptures using partial verses to defend and deliver Israel's doctrine:

> "*You got to do like the pharmacist who fills your prescription. You got to go over here in this jar and get a little bit, and you got to reach up here in this jar and get a little bit, and you got to reach down there in this jar and get a little bit. You put it all together, shake it up and you got what you need.*" Quoting:

Isaiah 28:9-10 "Whom shall he teach knowledge? and whom shall he make to understand doctrine? them that are weaned from the milk, and drawn from the breasts. For precept must be upon precept, precept upon precept; **line upon line, line upon line; here a little**, and **there a little**:"

The problem is that the above Scripture is being used out of context. The rhetoric no matter how beautifully delivered does not take into account the "Who, What, Why, When, Where and How" (The 5Ws and H). Actually it is drunkards' comments scoffing on Isaiah's writings.

Who does "Isaiah presume to teach knowledge? And **who does he take us to be** as if we were just weaned from the breast? For he is constantly repeating (**as if to little**

children), precept upon precept. Line (**rule or law**) upon line expresses the scorn of the imitators of Isaiah's speaking; he spoke *stammering* (**Isaiah 28:11**). God's manner of teaching confronts by its simplicity the pride of sinners. **The religious leaders are portrayed as staggering, vomiting drunkards and the people as sarcastic mockers of the prophet's message.** Since they rejected the Lord's offer of true peace, conditioned upon righteous living, He would send against them the Assyrians, whose foreign speech would serve as His mocking response to their jeering mimicry of the prophet."[4]

The pillar and foundational Scripture of which all of the doctrine of Israel centers is that in every generation God had a man to teach and lead His people Israel, quoting:

2 Chronicles 6:16 "Now therefore, O LORD God of Israel, keep with thy servant David my father that which thou hast promised him, saying, **There shall not fail thee a man in my sight to sit upon the throne of Israel;** yet so that thy children take heed to their way to walk in my law, as thou hast walked before me." (also **1 Kings 2:4; 8:25; 9:4-5**)

Ministers were expected to defend and to uphold this Biblical position. It was the glue and could not be questioned. In other words, this king man, was the mediator between God and His people Israel; his authority could not even be Biblically challenged. In order to begin to understand the issues with that premise, one would have to know something about Biblical and Church History which none of us study including the leadership in the organization:

- Biblically, the Israelites (in the Bible) failed the "**IF**" condition *(2 Chronicles 6:16; 1 Kings 2:4; 8:25; 9:4-5)*.

---

[4] Dockery, D. S., Butler, T. C., Church, C. L., Scott, L. L., Smith Ellis, M. A., and White, J. E. (1992). *Holman Bible Handbook* (p. 395). Nashville, Tennessee: Holman Bible Publishers.

- Israel went into captivity in **721** B.C. (approximately). **No More kings in Israel.**
- Judah went into captivity in **586** B.C. (approximately). **No More kings in Judah (until the birth of Jesus Christ).**
- 400 years of silence (intertestamental period), so no **Kings or Prophets**.
- Herod The Great's father, **Antipater I, was an Idumean** who **converted to Judaism** (the religion).
- Herod The Great was **a puppet King** (a Roman client king of Judea) **74/73** B.C – 4 B.C. He was not of Israelite or Judean ancestry. **He was not in the lineage of David**, but was the ruler of Judea, who ordered the **Massacre of the Innocents,** at the time of **the birth of Jesus**.
- The Romans divided up Herod the Great's kingdom upon his death. It went to his three sons, and they became tetrarchs (subordinate rulers). None of Herod's sons were in the lineage of David.
- The next true king in the lineage of David is Jesus. We are told in **Luke 1:31-33**:
- He will be great, and will be **called the Son of the Highest**;
- The Lord God will give Him **the throne of His father David**.
- **He will reign over the house of Jacob forever,**
- and of **His kingdom there will be no end."**

If there **is no end to Jesus Christ's Kingdom** (Isaiah 9:6-7; Luke 1:31-33) and He is **the King of Kings** (1 Timothy 6:15; Revelations 19:16), then **there could not possibly be** any other kings according to *(2 Chronicles 6:16;*

1 Kings 2:4; 8:25; 9:4-5). There is no Scripture justification for another king – physical or spiritual.

From the very pages of the 1st century manuscripts of John (**John 1:49 ESV**) we have Nathanael announcing, "...Rabbi, You are **the Son of God! You are the King of Israel!**"

The Spiritual Israel Church & Its Army was not established as an Ecclesiastical Corporation until nineteen hundred and thirty-seven years after Nathanael made his acknowledgement of Jesus as the king of Israel. However, the church attempted historical revisionism (an illegitimate distortion of the truth). The organization had a beginning just as so many other Christian groups who deviated from the truth of Scripture and ended up in the valley of the cults and false religions.

The organization was originally founded by Bishop Fred Derrick Fields and Bishop D. Dixson under the name "**The Israel of God's Church In David**" in the 1920s - 30s. It was in an Alabama gathering of a small band of believers, and it later was moved to Michigan. He claimed to be the ***God-Chosen King*** of "The Israel of God's Church In David." He stated in the first Manuscript of Rules and laws (The Blue Book Version, page 2)

- It pleased God for him to send out to the world the new **name**, **faith** and **doctrine** of His church.

- It pleased God who is the God of Israel to send "**the name**" that the God of Israel Himself gave His people, which was, is, and evermore shall be: **Israel**.

- The church which was, is, and ever shall be "**GOD'S CHURCH**."

- His people and church was, is, and evermore shall be "**IN DAVID**."

- We are not Israel because the Bible says Israel, **but we are Israel because the Spirit of God in us says we are Israel**.
- The Bible is our Witness that the Spirit within us is true.

According to Bishop Fred Derrick Fields, Manuscript – Rule (The Blue Book Version):

- Page 54: Ministers shall exhort and prove the doctrine by the Bible that Israel is the name for God's people to go in, be called, and the doctrine of the Israel of God's Church in David is God's **one and only way**. The minister must explain and prove all and the same to be true.
  - Notice there is no mention of Jesus Christ on that page; John 14:6 "*Jesus saith unto him, **I am the way, the truth, and the life**: no man cometh unto the Father, but by me.*"
- Page 60: The congregation was instructed to sing, "Blessed be the ties that bind our hearts in **Christian Love**."
  - Today, this is no longer done. In fact, Israel does not identify with Christians or believe that they are Christians. The word is not looked upon favorably.
  - The leadership of today teaches that Constantine started Christianity.
- Page 69: During the Marriage Ceremony the minister ended the ceremony in prayer, saying, "These and all other needed blessings we ask, according to Thy will, in the name **of Thy Son, Jesus Christ, Amen**."
  - Today, this is no longer done. In fact, **no prayers are done in Jesus' name**. All prayers

are done in the name of The God of Israel. Today, wherever possible, the leadership has struggled to replace **the name Jesus** with **the name Israel**. They've changed Christian songs that are sung in Israel using that approach. Some of the Bishops were suggesting that Israel needs its own Bible, but so far that has not materialized.

- Pages 70 - 71: The minister who preaches the funeral of one that was a member in Israel must wisely prove all these things according to the doctrine of Israel:
  - If an Israel member keeps God's sayings, then the Israel member **will never see death**.
    - The cornerstone Scripture used to support this teaching: **John 8:51** "Verily, verily, I say unto you, If a man keep my saying, he shall never see death."
  - But if an Israel member dies, then there is **hope for the dead**, although the Israel member may lose their body.
  - **Israel does not believe that you have to die**, but if you just happen to die as long as you "Own God's Name," then in Paradise God will prepare you a new body.
  - For Adam these words were said, and in him they are true. But in Christ if we love God, these are our words that He made new: From sin and death He came to save and **ransom Israel from the grave**, and **if His saying we keep**, the death in Adam **we shall never meet**. Then we might go most any day, but there will not be left the empty clay.

- Israel **does not believe** in **Heaven or Hell**. It is taught that both are a state of mind.
- When your loved ones die, as long as you live, they live in you.

- Pages 76 - 77: Ministers are instructed **"Do Not Preach Something you have Not Seen or Heard."** But take the Bible and **prove it by Every Other Good Way:**
    - That God has never **sent but one Man** in all past times and generations
    - To open and produce **His one and only way,**
    - and to make known and establish **His one and only Church.**
    - **Preach the Man** that God has sent in your generation. If any minister truly **studies the life of the Man** and how God led and taught him (**either they can get it from him or someone that has been with him**) and preach and prove it that God did truly send him, **the minister will be the most successful soul winner in Israel.**
        - It is not uncommon to hear bishops preach with the question and expected response of "No" to the following:
            - Did you see Jesus walk the water? <response **no**>
            - Did you see Jesus heal the blind? <response **no**>
            - Did you see Jesus turn water into wine? <response **no**>
            - Did you see Jesus make the lame man walk? <response **no**>

- Has anybody seen Jesus? <response **no**>
- But **the KING of Israel** (the man in this generation) you can see? <response **YES**>

No Minister is to preach any other doctrine except the doctrine of Israel. The minister must believe and prove all other doctrines are wrong.

- Page 80: **The King of Israel is the one and only man on earth** that **the true God of Israel talks to.** We are not to accept any other doctrine, faith, or leader.

- **If the King of Israel is WRONG**, then **we are lost**, world without end. But if the King of Israel is right, then we are saved with and in the doctrine that is only in him with an everlasting salvation. Therefore, be it known to all, **that if the God and doctrine in our King doesn't save us, we will never bow to another**.

- Any Minister in Israel **that has passed the third degree of the doctrine**, and if **they possess the power of the third degree in Israel**, and they have been endorsed and approved by the King, they have power in Israel to **"Forgive sins." (St John 20:21–23 ESV)**

  ○ "Forgiveness of sins is directed to a right relation or standing with God, a concern that in the Pauline letters would be called to justification, as for example in **Romans 3:21–5:11**. Accordingly, it is imperative to recognize that while Christians are involved in whatever mission the Holy Spirit assigns, it is God who ultimately does the forgiving.

    ▪ Christians who are thus involved in the forgiveness of sins **do so as agents of the Holy Spirit** and **never as independent

actors in this process. It is equally important to recognize that the Gospel of John, like the first epistle, is addressed to the church (the Christian community) and **not simply to individuals."** [5]

- "At first glance this is a remarkable statement that seems out of step with the role and authority of the disciples.
  - **It was not the disciples who could forgive sins but Jesus.** The literal reading from the Greek is more clear, stating: 'Those whose sins you forgive have already been forgiven; those whose sins you do not forgive have not been forgiven."
  - **God's forgiveness is not dependent upon human forgiveness,** but rather forgiveness is extended by God **as a result of individual responses to the proclamation of the gospel** by fellow human beings."[6]
  - "As they (Apostles) proclaimed the gospel, **they could honestly tell people who believed in that message that their sins were forgiven,** and **they could honestly tell people that did not believe in the message that their sins were not forgiven and that they stand condemned in God's eyes.** Jesus said, "Whoever believes in the Son has eternal life, but whoever rejects the Son will not see life, for God's wrath remains on him' (John 3:36)."[7]

---

[5] Borchert, G. L. (2002). *John 12–21* (Vol. 25B, p. 309). Nashville, TN: Broadman & Holman Publishers.

[6] Dockery, D. S., Butler, T. C., Church, C. L., Scott, L. L., Ellis Smith, M. A., White, J. E., (1992). *Holman Bible Handbook* (p. 630). Nashville, TN: Holman Bible Publishers.

[7] [http://www.gotquestions.org/John-20-23.html] (5/13/2016)

- **In Acts 8:18–25** Simon had sinned thinking he could purchase with money the gifts of God. Notice what the apostle Peter tells Simon and Simon's reply:

  Peter: Repent therefore of this thy wickedness, and **pray God, if perhaps the thought of thine heart may be forgiven thee.**

  Simon: "Then answered Simon, and said, **Pray ye to the Lord for me**, that none of these things which ye have spoken come upon me."

  Peter did not clear away Simon of his sins, and neither did Simon ask Peter to **forgive his sin**, but he asked the Apostle Peter to **pray to God for him** because of his sins.

- It is clearly taught in Scripture **that only God can forgive sins (Mark 2:7-8; Luke 5:21; Matthew 9:1-8):**
  - Jesus is both **fully God** and **fully Man**. He is the God Man.
  - He has two natures. John 1:1,14 (the Word was made flesh).
    - Greek **monogenes** [only begotten son]: "pertaining to being the only one of its kind or class, unique in kind." This is the meaning that is implied in John 3:16 (see also John 1:14, 18; 3:18; 1 John 4:9).
    - John was primarily concerned with demonstrating that Jesus is the Son of God (John 20:31), and he uses monogenes to highlight Jesus as uniquely God's Son—**sharing the same divine nature as God**—as opposed to believers who are **God's sons and daughters**

by adoption (Ephesians 1:5). Jesus is God's "one and only" Son. [8]

- **Acts 10: 43** "To him give all the prophets witness, that through his name whosoever believeth in him shall receive remission of sins." **(Colossians 2:13-14)**.

After Bishop Derrick Fields' death, **The Israel of God's Church In David** later split. Under the leadership of Bishop W.D. Dixson, **The Spiritual Israel Church & Its Army** (SICIA) emerged (he changed the name). It was established as an Ecclesiastical Corporation on May 9, 1938 under Bishop Dixson with signatures of 30 - 35 church members. It was said that this was done to conform to the laws and regulations of the land (the land of our captivity). **The Israel of God's Church in David** was never incorporated, but it was registered in October 25th 1948 under the Michigan Domestic Non-Profit Corporation (filing number 779140). The file status shows resolved.

The Preface in The Bylaws and Oracles of "The Spiritual Israel Church & Its Army" says:

> *the inward part of all men is spirit, and the spirit that dwelled in David **was Israel**. This **Spirit Israel** is **the foundation** upon which **God built His Church**. And all men who accept God's name **(Israel)** are united by a common purpose into a Spiritual Army.*

The above statement changes and derails the New Testament and its teachings on the gospel of Jesus Christ. The term "Spirit Israel" or "Spiritual Israel" does not exist in the Bible. It attempts to lay another foundation that is outside of Scripture and does so by presenting it as a new Revelation.

---

[8] http://www.gotquestions.org/only-begotten-son.html Retrieved 05-13-2016

- Mohammad did the same by claiming to receive revelation through Gabriel.
- Joseph Smith did the same by claiming to get revelation from the Father and Jesus Christ when he was a 14-year-old boy.

Matthew 16:18 "And I say also unto thee, That thou art Peter, **and upon this rock I will build my church;** and the gates of hell shall not prevail against it."

The Rock was what the Father revealed to **Peter "Thou art the Christ, the Son of the living God" (Matthew 16:16b). The rock** was the truth of who **Jesus Christ** actually is. **Jesus Christ** is the Foundation of the church (**1 Corinthians 3:11**)

Ephesians 2:20 "And are built upon the foundation of the apostles and prophets, Jesus Christ himself being the chief corner stone."

Even false organizations can thrive from the misled people that support their false doctrine as truth. In an Open Letter in The Bylaws and Oracles of "The Spiritual Israel Church & Its Army," pages 1 – 2, Bishop Robert Haywood, the King of Israel at that time, states how his predecessor, Archbishop Martin Tumpkin, **brought the church from 7 cent collections to an organization worth over two million dollars**. Bishop Haywood wrote on his pledge to fulfill the desire of Archbishop Tumpkin for the so-called **Black people to be recognized as a nation**, and to build a city on the land known as Israel Gardens, and to establish churches in each state in The United States of America. He appealed to each member to adhere to the laws set forth in the book (The Bylaws and Oracles). By doing so they would be doing their part to build God's Kingdom on Earth.

- Reportedly, in 1972, Muhammad told followers that the Nation of Islam had a net worth of $75 million.[9]
- *Time* magazine estimated in 1996 that the **Mormon LDS church's** assets exceeded **$30 billion**[10]
- Others such as Word of Faith Movement preachers don't readily disclose their net-worth. But it is a big business in the Church.

The Bylaws and Oracles of "The Spiritual Israel Church & Its Army" Article 26 states: All members who address the congregation during any religious service MUST first repeat the following saying, "**I rise and give honor to the Holy Father, The King of All Israel.**"

- At the time that I joined the church, it was mandatory to say: "**I rise and give honor to the Holy Father, The King of All Israel, Bishop Robert Haywood.**" But years later we were allowed to drop his name from this saying.
- Article 31: All persons (members and visitors a like) **MUST stand** when the **King of All Israel** comes into the sanctuary and approaches the altar to address the congregation.
- All ministers were instructed to stay in (preach from) The Seven Seals of Spiritual Israel Church.
  - Israel doctrine preached The Seven Seals. No one ever told us how they became the Seven Seals. But what I can say is that they were Scriptures that supported the doctrine of Israel.

---

[9] Evanzz, Karl. The Messenger: *The Rise and Fall of Elijah Muhammad* Random House, 2001.

[10] Biema, David Van. (August 4, 1997). *Kingdom Come"* 150 (5). Time Magazine. Retrieved September 2, 2006.

- No one could ever accuse Israel of not using Scriptures, because (We) the preachers would bombard you with a ton of Scriptures in attack mode. What I didn't know then was that the majority were skewed and taken out of context. If you learned them, you were elevated and you taught and preached them to others. You were equipped to defend Israel's Doctrine. You didn't read other books such as books on church history.
- The Seven Seals were the evidence Scriptures (108) used to prove that Israel was the only way, God's people were called Israel, God only promised to save Israel, God's name was Israel, and that you had to surname yourself by the name of Israel (change your name).
- Ministers were encouraged and admonished to use **St. John 7: 37-38** as their first Scripture when preaching:

  In the last day, that great day of the feast, ***Jesus stood and cried****, saying, If any man thirst, let him come unto me, and drink.* ***He that believeth on me, as the Scripture*** *hath said, out of his belly shall flow rivers of living water.*

- The minister would say something like*: "Well, Jesus ain't standing before you today, but I am standing before you crying.* ***Believe on me as I prove it by the Scriptures*** *and* ***if I don't prove it by the Scriptures, you don't have to believe it****. But if I do, out of the belly of your mind is going to flow peace, joy, and happiness...."*

- If you were to try to preach about Jesus Christ, you would be reprimanded, and instructed to stay in the seals.

Israel preached that our problem was that we, the black people, didn't know who we were. The King of Israel would say that he came after us, to get us, and to teach us who we really are by saying, "*You are not darkies, spooks, jigaboos, negroes, niggers, or colored people. Your nationality is Ethiopian and your spiritual name is Israel.*" Quoting:

> **Amos 9:7** "**Are ye not as children of the Ethiopians** unto me, **O children of Israel**? saith the LORD. Have not I brought up Israel out of the land of Egypt? and the Philistines from Caphtor, and the Syrians from Kir?"

- This verse, when read in context, was about judgement and not name declaring or defining. God is just and not a respecter of persons.
- Just as God had delivered Israel, He also delivered other nations, but just as He had punished those nations for their sins, He would punish Israel for her sins.
- God's involvement with Israel does not immunize them from judgment any more than His involvement with any nation immunizes it from judgment. (**Amos 1:1-8; Deuteronomy 2:5-23**)

"How come you didn't know this?" the minister would ask during his rhetoric, eager to wittingly give the answer:

> "*They have said, Come, and **let us cut them off from being a nation**; that **the name of Israel** may be no more in remembrance*" **Psalm 83:4.**

- When read in context, this was talking about the Edomites, Ishmaelites, Moabites, Amalekites, Gebalites, Ammonites, Assyrians, and Philistines. These were surrounding nations of Judah that formed a coalition against Judah (Israel here is the common name).

- When in history did America ever form an alliance with any other nations against the nation of Ethiopia (Africa)? In fact, it was the Africans that sold other Africans to the Muslim slave traders.

- Once in America, our ancestors were cut off from **THE Nation of Ethiopia**, their names changed, and they were treated brutally, but it is a long stretch to read the Black man into this Scripture.

- The slave trade is another matter and many countries had a hand in this act, but it is still not related to this Scripture.

Ministers would learn and commit to memory every Scripture that used the word "black, dark, Ethiopia, etc." to promote and defend the doctrine of Israel.

Jeremiah 13:23-24 "Can the Ethiopian change his skin, or the leopard his spots? *then* may ye also do good, that are accustomed to do evil. Therefore will I scatter them as the stubble that passeth away by the wind of the wilderness.

But this Scripture was not given by God as a wake up call to identity, but of the Jews habit of sinning.

- "**23. Ethiopian**—the Cushite of Abyssinia. Habit is second nature; as therefore it is morally impossible that **the Jews** can alter their inveterate habits of sin, nothing remains but the infliction of the extremist punishment, their expatriation (Je 13:24). **24.** (Ps 1:4)." [11]

- "Just as persons cannot change their skin color or a leopard its spots, **so the people could not change their propensity for evil.** The darkness of

---

[11] Jamieson, R., Fausset, A. R., & Brown, D. (1997). *Commentary Critical and Explanatory on the Whole Bible* (Vol. 1, p. 520). Oak Harbor, WA: Logos Research Systems, Inc.

judgment would descend on the incorrigible nation, and the people would be swept away into exile like chaff before the wind." [12]

Job 30:30 My skin is black upon me, and my bones are burned with heat.

- "**30:30** Verse 30 unquestionably describes Job's diseased skin. **It was "black" and "peeled," or literally, "My skin grows black from off me."** [13]
    - In the second line it was literally his "bones" that burned with fever. "Skin" and "bones" are both metonymies for "body."
    - These last symptoms of Job's malady must be taken with others to complete the picture of his intense physical discomfort. He had scabs and festering sores over his entire body (7:5), malnutrition (17:7; 19:20), a repulsive appearance (19:19), bad breath (19:17), and pain day and night (30:17). Neither his condition nor his attitude toward God had improved."

The minister would ask who it was that you knew that was cut off from being a nation and brought to America, the Black Man! Quoting:

Acts 7:6 "And God spake on this wise, **That his seed should sojourn in a strange land**; and that they should **bring them into bondage**, and **entreat them evil four hundred years.**"

- When read in context, *God Made Promises to Abraham (7:2–8)*. Stephen summarizes the covenant that God made with Abraham. **In the holy land, Abraham never had or owned a "foot of ground."**

---

[12] Chisholm, R. B. (1998). The Major Prophets. In D. S. Dockery (Ed.), *Holman concise Bible commentary* (p. 298). Nashville, TN: Broadman & Holman Publishers.

[13] Alden, R. L. (1993). *Job* (Vol. 11, p. 297). Nashville, TN: Broadman & Holman Publishers.

Abraham received the promises outside of the Holy Land. "Stephen was providing a critique of the narrow Jewish nationalism **that confined God to the land of Israel** and particularly to the temple."[14]

- "The four hundred years ran from about 1845 to 1445 B.C., from the original enslavement in Egypt to the year of Exodus." [15]

The minister of Israel would preach that we were sold to the Grecians and brought from Africa to America:

Joel 3:6 "The children also of Judah and the children of Jerusalem have **ye sold unto the Grecians**, that ye might **remove them far from their border.**"

- "Phoenician and Philistine involvement in slave trade (v. 6) is mentioned elsewhere (cf. Amos 1:6, 9). According to Arvid S. Kapelrud, professor and Biblical scholar of the Old Testament, the Greeks mentioned here are actually Ionians (*yewānîm*), who populated the coasts of Asia Minor (*Joel Studies*, p. 154). Ionian commerce was at its peak in the seventh and sixth centuries B.C. Ezekiel 27:13, 19 mentions Tyrian trading arrangements (including slaves) with the Ionians (or Greece). The trading recalled in Joel may have occurred in conjunction with Judah's fall to the Babylonians."[16]

- "The main point is that the Philistines and Phoenicians followed a **deliberate policy of**

---

[14] Polhill, J. B. (1998). Acts. In D. S. Dockery (Ed.), *Holman Concise Bible Commentary* (p. 508). Nashville, TN: Broadman & Holman Publishers.

[15] Gangel, K. O. (1998). *Acts* (Vol. 5, p. 104). Nashville, TN: Broadman & Holman Publishers.

[16] Chisholm, R. B., Jr. (1985). Joel. In J. F. Walvoord & R. B. Zuck (Eds.), *The Bible Knowledge Commentary: An Exposition of the Scriptures* (Vol. 1, pp. 1421–1422). Wheaton, IL: Victor Books.

banishing Jews from their homeland. Put in modern terms, they were practicing '**ethnic cleansing**' in hopes that they could solve their version of the '**Jewish problem.**' This text, in other words, was an early example of the treatment Jews would have to suffer for centuries to come."[17]

According to the doctrine of Israel, it is preached that we are the real Israelites and the real Jews:

Revelation 2:9 "I know thy works, and tribulation, and poverty, (but thou art rich) and **I know the blasphemy of them which say they are Jews, and are not, but are the synagogue of Satan.**"

- "This striking note **condemns the Jews who met for worship in Smyrna.** Because **they were slandering the Christians**, their meeting had become a 'synagogue of Satan' rather than a synagogue of God.

  o Note the implication: just as those in Smyrna who claimed to be God's people, **the Jews, proved by their actions they were not worthy** of the name, so those who claim to be God's people, **the Christians, can prove by their actions** to be the '**church of Satan**'."[18]

- "Their detractors falsely claim to be *Jews*. What does this mean? We must keep in mind the fact that John, the writer of Revelation, is himself a Jew.

  o The term may be used in the literal sense of people of the Jewish race, and given the large

---

[17] Garrett, D. A. (1997). *Hosea, Joel* (Vol. 19A, pp. 383–384). Nashville, TN: Broadman & Holman Publishers.

[18] Easley, K. H. (1998). *Revelation* (Vol. 12, p. 37). Nashville, TN: Broadman & Holman Publishers.

number of Jews in Smyrna, it is probable that these are Jews.

- o But in denying their claim to be '**Jews**,' John is using the word in the extended sense of "God's (chosen) people," which Jews claimed to be.

- o **For him it is the Christians**, and not the Jews, **who are the chosen people** (see Paul's definition of authentic Jews in Rom 2:28–29; 9:8; Gal 6:15–16). **John's position is that Christians are the true people of God.** If translators feel that translating *Jews* literally will give the wrong impression to readers, it will be helpful to say "those who say (claim) to be God's people, but are not.

- These Jews in the ethnic sense are not Jews in the spiritual sense (also 3:9); they are *a synagogue of Satan*. John purposely uses the Jewish term *synagogue* (also 3:9), the name for a group of Jews meeting in one place for religious purposes. The phrase *of Satan* means either that they belong to Satan, or else that they serve Satan instead of serving God (see **John 8:44**)."[19]

The minister would ask the congregation, "Who is it today that enters the synagogues?" Then he would answer quoting:

Revelation 3:9 "Behold, I will make them of the synagogue of Satan, which **say they are Jews, and are not, but do lie**; behold, **I will make them to come and worship before thy feet, and to know that I have loved thee.**"

---

[19] Bratcher, R. G., & Hatton, H. (1993). *A handbook on the Revelation to John* (p. 47). New York: United Bible Societies.

The minister building his case would say, "But this is the real Jew referring to:

Romans 2:28-29 "For **he is not a Jew, which is one outwardly**; neither is that circumcision, which is outward in the flesh: But he is a Jew, **which is one inwardly**; and circumcision is that of the heart, in the spirit, and not in the letter; **whose praise is not of men, but of God.**"[i]

- "In the Old Testament, circumcision was outwardly in the flesh and a sign of belonging to Yahweh **(Genesis 17:9-14; Joshua 5:2-12)**.
- In the New Testament, circumcision is the stripping off of a carnal nature, and the complete removal of moral depravity, and this is done by Christ Jesus **(Colossians 2:11; 3:9)**""[20]

It is taught in Israel that somebody beat us to our mailbox and got our letter (the Bible), but that it takes a man of understanding to draw it out. According to the doctrine of Israel, this man is the King of Israel who was sent to wake us up from sleep as to who we are, as found in:

Proverbs 20:5 "Counsel in the heart of man is like deep water; **but a man of understanding will draw it out.**"

The ministers would teach and defend that Jesus had to be black because the Bible said his hair was "like wool;" pulling the congregation into the error because he'd ask, "who do you know beside the black man that has nappy wooly hair;" quoting:

---

[20] Lavender, Malcom L. *Lavender's New Testament*, A Literal Translation of Robinson-Pierpont Majority Text (1995)

Revelation 1:14 "His head and his hairs were **white like wool, as white as snow**; and his eyes were as a flame of fire;"

- Simply stated, the emphasis was not on the texture of the hair, but the color; "**white like**," "**as**," "white like wool," "white like snow."
  - No, the text does not imply that his hair was nappy like a black man,
  - No, his eyes were not blood-shot like a wino,
  - No, his feet were not ashy like a black who had just taken a bath.
  - And let me ask when was the last time you saw a black man with a **switch-blade** coming out of his mouth?
- "**Among the lampstands** John saw **Someone** 'like a Son of Man,' an expression used in **Daniel 7:13** to refer to Christ.
  - The description was that of a priest **dressed in a** long **robe ... with a golden sash around his chest (Revelation 1:13).**
    - **The whiteness of His hair** corresponded to that of the Ancient of Days (cf. Dan. 7: 9), a reference to God the Father. God the Son has the same purity and eternity as God the Father, as signified by *the whiteness* of **His head and hair.**
    - The **eyes like blazing fire** described His piercing judgment of sin (cf. **Revelation 2:18**).
    - This concept is further enhanced by **His feet** which **were like bronze glowing in a furnace** (cf. 2:18). The bronze altar in the

temple was related to sacrifice for sin and divine judgment on it.

- **His voice** was compared to the roar **of rushing waters.**
- **His face** glowed with a brilliance **like the sun shining.** John noticed that **in His right hand He held seven stars**, described in verse 20 as the angels or messengers of the seven churches. Significantly Christ held them in His right hand, indicating sovereign possession.
  - Speaking of Christ's role as a Judge, John saw a **sharp double-edged sword** coming **out of His mouth.** This type of sword (*rhomphaia*, also referred to in 2:12, 16; 6:8; 19:15, 21) was used by the Romans in a stabbing action designed to kill.
  - Jesus Christ was no longer a Baby in Bethlehem or a Man of sorrows crowned with thorns. He was now the Lord of glory."[21]

The ministers would teach and falsely defend that Solomon said that **he was black**, when in actuality it was a woman that made the statement in the Song of Solomon. Quoting:

Song of Solomon 1:5 "**I am black, but comely**, O ye daughters of Jerusalem, as the tents of Kedar, as the curtains of Solomon."

- "In the **Song of Solomon chapter 1**: there are "three singing parts are evident: a male, a female, and a female chorus.

---

[21] Walvoord, John F. (1985). Revelation. In J. F. Walvoord & R. B. Zuck (Eds.), *The Bible Knowledge Commentary: An Exposition of the Scriptures* (Vol. 2, pp. 930–931). Wheaton, IL: Victor Books.

- The three take turns singing their parts, but they do not follow a consistent sequence. At times it is difficult to tell who is singing a given line or strophe of lyrics because the Hebrew text does not delineate the parts. Usually, however, **it is self-evident from the gender of the pronouns used** and other explicit details."[22]
    - The Shulamite Girl: verses 1-4, 5-7, 12-14, 16-17
    - The Daughters of Jerusalem: verses 4,11
    - The Beloved: 8 -10,15
- 1:5-6 "Unlike the pale court ladies, the rustic Shulamite has spent much time in **the sun** as **a keeper of the vineyards**. Hence she is **tanned** and **dark, but lovely**."[23]
- 1:5-6. "The beloved's suntanned appearance (**dark am I**) revealed that she worked in the fields. This made her feel insecure (**do not stare at me**) among the city dwellers and in particular the women of Jerusalem.
    - **She compared her dark skin** to **the tents of Kedar**, which were made of black goats' hair. The people of Kedar were nomads in northern Arabia who descended from Ishmael (**Gen. 25:13**). They were known for their archery (Isa. 21:16-17) and flocks (Isa. 60:7; Jer. 49:28-29; Ezek. 27:21; also see Ps. 120:5; Isa. 42:11; Jer. 2:10). Apparently **the tent curtains of Solomon** were also black.

---

[22] Garrett, D. A. (1993). *Proverbs, Ecclesiastes, Song of Songs* (Vol. 14, p. 384). Nashville, TN: Broadman & Holman Publishers.

[23] MacDonald, W. (1995). *Believer's Bible Commentary: Old and New Testaments.* (A. Farstad, Ed.) (p. 922). Nashville, TN: Thomas Nelson.

- o **Her explanation for her dark appearance** was almost an apology. Because of hard outdoor work in **the vineyards**, required of her by her brothers, she was forced to neglect the cultivation of her **own vineyard**, that is, herself and her appearance (cf. Song 8:12)."[24]

The ministers falsely reading into Scripture that black people are the true Israelites, and that your nationality is Ethiopian and your Spiritual name is Israel, Quoting:

Psalm 68:31 "Princes shall come out of Egypt; **Ethiopia shall soon stretch out her hands unto God.**"

- It is difficult for many African-Americans (black people) to accept the fact that Ethiopia, no matter how great she was, was a gentile nation. The verse is prophetically saying that this gentile nation, **Ethiopia,** will soon humble herself and submit to the God of Israel. We get many Scriptural examples:

- **Isaiah 45:14 "Thus saith the Lord**, The labour of Egypt, **and merchandise of Ethiopia** and of the Sabeans, **men of stature, shall come over unto thee**, and they shall be thine: they shall come after thee; in chains they shall come over, and they shall fall down unto thee, they shall make supplication unto thee, saying, **Surely God is in thee; and there is none else, there is no God.**"

- **Zephaniah 3:10** "From beyond the rivers of Ethiopia my suppliants, even the daughter of my dispersed, shall bring mine offering."

---

[24] Deere, J. S. (1985). Song of Songs. In J. F. Walvoord & R. B. Zuck (Eds.), *The Bible Knowledge Commentary: An Exposition of the Scriptures* (Vol. 1, pp. 1012–1013). Wheaton, IL: Victor Books.

- "Princes of Egypt and **Ethiopia submit to God's will**. David is predicting the spread of Messiah's kingdom among the Gentiles." [25]

- "**Even Ethiopia, that had stretched out her hands against God's Israel (2 Chronicles 14:9-14), should now** *stretch out her hands unto God,* **in prayer**, in presents, and to take hold on him, and that soon. *Agree with thy adversary quickly.* Out of all nations some shall be gathered in to Christ and be owned by him.[26]

- **Ethiopia was an ally to Israel against the king of Assyria: 2 Kings 19:9-10** And when he heard say of **Tirhakah king of Ethiopia**, Behold, he is come out to fight against thee: he sent messengers again unto Hezekiah, saying, Thus shall ye speak to **Hezekiah king of Judah**, saying, Let not thy God in whom thou trustest deceive thee, saying, Jerusalem shall not be delivered into the hand of the **king of Assyria**."

In the proper context, using hermeneutics it is clearly understandable, Biblically, that there were Ethiopian converts to Judaism whether through marriage or choice. But that is totally different from stealing someone's ethnic identity and historical revisionism.

- Moses, an **Israelite,** Married an **Ethiopian** Woman (**Numbers 12:1**).

- Ebed-Melech the **Ethiopian** eunuch saves Jeremiah the Prophet (**an Israelite**) from death in the dungeon (Jeremiah 38:7-13).

---

[25] Smith, J. E. (1996). *The Wisdom Literature and Psalms* (Ps 68:30–31). Joplin, MO: College Press Pub. Co.

[26] Henry, M. (1994). *Matthew Henry's Commentary on the Whole Bible: Complete and Unabridged in One Volume* (p. 840). Peabody, MA: Hendrickson.

- God delivers Ebed-Melech the **Ethiopian** eunuch because he put his trust in **Israel's God (Jeremiah 39:15-18)**.
- An **Ethiopian** eunuch convert (proselyte) to **Judaism** had come to Jerusalem to worship. Notice, the Ethiopian convert was reading a manuscript of Isaiah but was not understanding what he was reading.
  - Phillip, who was not only an Israelite, was a follower of Jesus Christ who makes clear the text by preaching Jesus beginning at the same Scripture the Ethiopian eunuch was reading.
  - The **Ethiopian** eunuch convert immediately **wants to convert from the religion of Judaism to become a Christian** (a follower of Jesus Christ). **Acts 8:27-39**.
  - He came to Jerusalem because of one religion and was converted to true religion.

The King of Israel has (unchallenged) rule, and he can't be removed from office. His words are final in all matters spiritual, doctrine, dogma, and credence.

Israel taught that the **Lord is a man** and not a Spirit because a Spirit **can't shave** and the preacher would reference *Isaiah 7:20* "*In the same day shall the Lord shave with a razor……*" And that **the Lord is a man of war** (*Exodus 15:3*). If it was the King preaching, he would point to his beard and say something like, "I sure shaved this morning, and I am warring with all of your conditions." If the doors of the church were open, the preacher's job was to show all why you had to change your name to Israel and would have these Scriptures read as he expounded on them:

Genesis 35:10 "And God said unto him, Thy name is Jacob: thy name shall not be called any more Jacob,

but Israel shall be thy name: and he called his name Israel."

The preacher would give examples like: if your name was Baptist, Catholic, Methodist, Presbyterian whatever it is, you needed to change it to Israel.

"One shall say, I am the LORD's; and another shall call himself by the name of Jacob; **and another shall subscribe with his hand** unto the LORD, **and surname himself by the name of Israel.**" Isaiah **44:5**.

"What does 'subscribe' mean?" the preacher would ask. To give. "And what does 'surname' mean?" the preacher would ask. It means to change. And then he would bellow, "Who said it?" as the readers read:

"Thus saith the LORD the King of Israel, and his redeemer the LORD of hosts; I am the first, and I am the last; and **beside me there is no God.**" Isaiah **44:6**.

It would be shown that both **the father** and **the Son**'s name was **Israel** using the Scripture out of context of its original meaning and intent. This Scripture would be read to show that the father is Israel and that if the God of Israel is your Father then you should be called Israel too. Most children, unless they are bastards, take on their father's name it would be expounded. The minister would rhetorically work these verses over the congregation. You would be transformed to a place over time that you knew exactly what Scripture was next and could repeat what would be said before it was said. But, never realizing that we were being programed (indoctrinated).

- **Genesis 49:2** "Gather yourselves together, and hear, ye sons of Jacob; and **hearken unto Israel your father.**"

- o But isn't there a big difference between the use of "**F**"ather and "**f**"ather?
- o A heavenly **Father** and an earthly father?
- o Was this Jacob (Israel) or God speaking in the verse?

If the father's name is Israel, then the Son's name has got to be Israel. "Doesn't your son take on your last name?" the minister would ask.

- **Exodus 4:22** "And thou shalt say unto Pharaoh, Thus saith the LORD, **Israel is my Son**, even my firstborn:"
- **Hosea 11:1** "When **Israel was a child**, then I loved him, and **called my son out of Egypt**."
- **Matthew 2:6** "And thou Bethlehem, in the land of Juda, art not the least among the princes of Juda: for out of thee shall come a Governor, **that shall rule my people Israel**."

The Preacher would close his sermon by saying, "If you are not serving the God of Israel, you are not serving a real God," as he extended his hands for those he had shook from the tree.

Israel's Doctrine in a nutshell on Jesus Christ: We were taught that He was not doing anything else:

John 17:4 "I have glorified thee on the earth: **I have finished the work** which thou gavest me to do."

The preacher would ask the congregation to spell the word "**FINISHED**." "What does the word finished mean?" the preacher would ask. "It means '**through**.' Jesus said He is not doing anything else."

WHAT WAS NOT TAUGHT IN ISRAEL:

Israel did teach that that there were things that The God of Israel hated:

Proverbs 6:16-19 "These six things doth the Lord hate: yea, seven are an abomination unto him: A proud look, a lying tongue, and hands that shed innocent blood, An heart that deviseth wicked imaginations, feet that be swift in running to mischief, A false witness that speaketh lies, and he that soweth discord among brethren."

But nothing was taught on fornication, adultery, or homosexuality. In fact, many times idolatry and adultery were confused and simply explained as putting something before the God of Israel or making other gods out of your wife, car, children, money, home, etc.

- Nothing was stressed about saving one's self for marriage.
- No focus on letting each man have his own wife to avoid fornication. (**1 Corinthians 7:1-5**).
- No focus on let each woman have her own husband to avoid fornication. (**1 Corinthians 7: 1-5**).
- Implied does not equate to practice.

In Israel there was order to the services and structure:

- The King, Bishops, Elders, Reverends, and Evangelists in color uniformed robes white or black (depending on the service) sitting together.
- The Deacons and Jr. Deacons uniformed (black suit, white shirt and black tie and shoes) sitting appropriately together.
- The Mother's board and Daughter's board uniformed (white dress [below knee], stocking, shoes, and hankie) sitting appropriately together.

- The women who sat on the front row would have scarves to dress over their laps to maintain decency.

When I came into Israel I was very zealous with the new doctrine I was learning. Although it is preached that Israel is not new, it was new to me. The Scripture verses with Israel and the way they were expounded on was new to me. No one had ever shown me Israel in the Bible and made Scriptures resonate with me. Also there was a relationship with all the new brothers and sisters that I was meeting who were becoming my spiritual family.

I remember on a few occasions running into some people in the streets who knew about and had been raised in Israel, but they had left the organization. They would say, "I know all about Israel," but their words would never be anything about the doctrine. They would tell me about who had been sleeping with who, and who was married but had fathered children by other sisters in the church. They would tell me of things that they had seen in the church as children and why they left Israel. At that time, this was not what I wanted to hear. I would tell myself that they don't know about the doctrine of Israel. I swore nothing would ever make me leave Israel, but what I didn't know is that I didn't know the doctrine either. I was taught that Israel was a way of life, and I was along for the ride. Nothing could tell me that I was in the wrong place because The God of Israel had delivered me from drugs.

I am not implying that everyone in Israel was vain and void of integrity. But just like me, they were there; sound doctrine or not, integrity or not. The problem was that Israel did not address the issue of fidelity. Children were born out of wedlock, fornication, and adultery. Scriptures related to these subjects were glossed over, if touched at all. Even if you read it yourself, every thing or meaning was so spiritualized that you were always seeking justification for an action or self-deception – "The God of Israel knows my heart," was a constant phrase used by many of us.

- I do know of cases where a mother or daughter who had a baby out of wedlock resigned from the board.
- I never saw or heard of a minister or deacon resigning for having a child or two out of wedlock,
    - Or committing adultery or fornication.
    - Some of these men were leaders.
    - We knew, but how can one cast the mote out of his brother's eye when you have a beam in your own eye?
- Everyone just served the God of Israel, who forgave us of our sins. The term "practicing sinner" was a term I never heard until after leaving Israel.

As long as you didn't put anything before the God of Israel and you carried Him with you everywhere you went, you were straight. There is no Seal within the Seven Seals that deals with sexual conduct. Of course you were instructed every now and then to love your wife, but I cannot remember a service or theme that focused or taught on the subject of "**pornea,**" (see Glossary for meaning). Lesson Guides were generated each year and sent to each temple in "**The Spiritual Israel Church & Its Army.**" There was a theme, subject and scripture related to the theme so that all temples would be on one teaching, one accord, "Israel."

Tell young men that have just come out of the streets that as long as you don't put anything in front of serving The God of Israel, you can have what you want. It may not have been said in those exact words, but when you don't teach sound doctrine and leave room for those taught under you to fill in the blanks, it is a disaster waiting to happen. One Bishop at least that I remember used to allude to this Scripture:

> **Isaiah 4:1** "And in that day **seven women shall take hold of one man**, saying, We will eat our own bread,

and wear our own apparel: only let us be called by thy name, to take away our reproach."

Without Biblical context, what does it suggest to you at first glance? Sometimes it was taught that it was not how many wives and concubines King Solomon had, but the problem was that he allowed them to turn his heart away from The God of Israel and he built altars to their idol gods (**1 Kings 11:1-13**).

- But the text says he disobeyed God **1 Kings 11:2-4**. He did what God told him not to do, and allowed them to do what God said should not be done.

- The text says Solomon did evil in the sight of the Lord (**1 Kings 11:6).**

- If wives and **concubines** didn't work for Solomon, the wisest man on earth what would make us believe it would work for us?
  - We would say mockingly, just because you can only eat one pork-chop, don't get mad at me because I can eat two or three. But there is no Scriptural basis given for this.

- The Scripture teaches that David committed adultery and murder, but we choose to remember Scripture that teaches that he was a man after God's Own Heart.

ISRAEL THE CHURCH OF THE FIRST BORN:

Next is the Doctrine of Israel as taught by the late Bishop Martin Tumpkin, the 3rd King in The Spiritual Israel Church & Its Army. Excerpts are transcribed word for word, where possible, from a LP live recording of his sermon, titled "Israel, The Church of the First Born," at Temple No 1 located at 9375 Amity St. in Detroit, MI 48214 on Sunday, May 16, 1971. It was under the supervision of Senator Bristoe Bryant,

Religious Director of Radio Station WJLB in Detroit, Michigan. While I could not capture the spirit of his delivery, the essence of what was being articulated through eisegesis of Scripture is present:

> "Thanking God for enabling us to return back to the House of Israel, Temple No. 1, to give thanks and praise to His Holy Name. Thankful for each and every one that is out on time showing that you are seeking for more wisdom, knowledge, and understanding of a true and living God.
>
> And to our visitors, we want you to know that this is your church, and if you have never been here before, you have the privilege tonight of being in the church of the First Born, which is written in heaven and not in the sky. Heaven is in you, and it is written in heaven. And it is being brought forth in every generation that you may have a right back to the tree of life. It was in the beginning, and God named it before the foundation of the world.
>
> When Jesus came on the scene, He knew that the church, the firstborn church, had got lost. Because He, Jesus, was back there in the beginning when it was made. He preached that God has blessed us with all spiritual blessing in heavenly places in Christ **(Ephesians 1:3).** *Heavenly places in Christ*, not in the sky. The birds fly in the firmaments of heaven and they fly right down here on the ground. Heavenly places don't have to be above the sun, moon, and stars.
>
> But the ***general assembly*** and ***church of the firstborn***, which are written in heaven **(Hebrews 12:23)** and if it is written in heaven, wherever it is wrote at is where the heavenly places must be. God said "I will put my laws into their mind, and **write them in their hearts**" **(Hebrews 8:10)** and **in their minds will I write them (Hebrews 10:16).** So in the

heavenly places is where the church is to be wrote. God chose Israel before the foundation of the world **(Ephesians 1:4)**. Because of this, we ought to want to know what was it that God chose to be written in us and what is His name. Since God chose Israel before the foundation of the world **(Isaiah 44:1)**, you are a special people unto Himself. He said you only of all the families of the earth have I known **(Amos 3:2)**

And because God was so concerned about you, he said in,

> **Hosea 4:1-2** "Hear the word of the LORD, **ye children of Israel: for the Lord hath a controversy with the inhabitants of the land, because there is no truth, nor mercy, nor knowledge of God in the land.** By swearing, and lying, and killing, and stealing, and committing adultery, they break out, and blood toucheth blood."

When God saw that His people had strayed off into idolism, He called His son out of Egypt. Because He heard the moans and groans of the children of Israel in Egypt. He called Moses and said, 'I'm going to send you to Egypt.' The question is how come God when he heard them he didn't go himself?

> **Amos 3:7** 'Surely the Lord God will do **nothing**, but he revealeth his secret unto his servants the prophets.'

Well God, where did You send Your prophet?

> **Ezekiel 33:7** 'So thou, O son of man, **I have set thee a watchman unto the house of Israel**; therefore thou shalt **hear the word at my mouth**, and **warn them from me**.'

What am I to warn you today? I am not called to ascend into the heaven, or to bring Christ down from above, and neither below, to bring up Christ again from the dead. But what saith it? The word is nigh thee, even in thy mouth. If you want the church to be built up in you, you're going to have to eat and drink my words.

Oh Israel, ain't you glad that one day you came to the house of Israel and sat down and listened to what God said through His body.

We're living in the last days; we're living in the days of the son of man. And as it were in the **days of Noah, so** will be the coming of the Son of Man.

> **Micah 4:1-2** 'But in the last days it shall come to pass, that the mountain of the house of the **Lord shall be established in the top of the mountains**, and it shall be exalted above the hills; and **people shall flow unto it**. And **many nations shall come**, and say, Come, and **let us go up to** the mountain of the Lord, and **to the house of the God of Jacob**;'

Let us see then what is the name of house of Jacob:

> **Genesis 28: 20-22** 'And Jacob vowed a vow, saying, **If God will be with me, and will keep me in this way that I go,** and will give me bread to eat, and raiment to put on, So that I come again to my father's house in peace; **then shall the Lord be my God: And this stone, which I have set for a pillar**, shall be God's house:....'

Let us see what is the name of the stone:

> **Genesis 49:24** 'But his bow abode in strength, and the arms of his hands were made strong by the hands of the mighty God of Jacob; (from thence is the shepherd, **the stone of Israel**).'

If the stone is Israel, then the foundation has to be Israel. As time moved forth they saw that the house of Israel was prospering too fast. They said let us cut them off from being a nation:

> **Psalms 83: 4** 'They have said, Come, and let us cut them off from being a nation; **that the name of Israel may be no more in remembrance.**'

But God heard them. He heard what they said. And God said:

> **Acts 4:11-12** '**This is the stone** which was set at nought of you builders, **which is become the head of the corner. Neither is there salvation in any other:** for **there is none other name under heaven given among men, whereby we must be saved.**'

As time moved on God wanted them to see that they would not have to go all over the world looking for a man to come to redeem you and he said in

> **Isaiah 41:25a** '**I have raised up one from the north**, and he shall come: from the rising of the sun **shall he call upon my name....**'

Everybody knows who my father's name is and I find that it says:

> **Isaiah 44:6** '**Thus saith the Lord the King of Israel**, and his redeemer the Lord of hosts; **I am the first, and I am the last**; and **beside me there is no God.**'

Aren't you glad that you're called by your Father's name, because He named you before the foundation of the world. And when you got lost from that name, I find that He loved you so much that He said unto the son:

> **John 3:16** 'For God so loved the world, **that he gave his only begotten Son, that whosoever**

> **believeth in him should not perish**, but have everlasting life.'

What was in Him? And when Jesus began to preach to them he said, I want you to know what is in me:

> **John 14:10a** 'Believest thou not that I am in the Father, **and the Father in me?**'

Well Jesus, what is Your father's name? I find that He said:

> **1 Chronicles 17:24** 'Let it even be established, that thy name may be magnified for ever, saying, **The Lord of hosts is the God of Israel, even a God to Israel:**'

As time moved on, after Jesus had come forth He let them know in:

> **Matthew 15:24** 'But he answered and said, **I am not sent but unto the lost sheep of the house of Israel.**'

And the book of Acts picked it up, that after they had got lost from that name:

> **Acts 7:6** 'And God spake on this wise, That **his seed should sojourn in a strange land**; and that **they should bring them into bondage**, and **entreat them evil four hundred years.**'

Who was His seed, Paul picked it up:

> **Romans 11:1-2a** 'I say then, Hath God cast away his people? God forbid. **For I also am an Israelite**, of the seed of Abraham, of the tribe of Benjamin. **God hath not cast away his people which he foreknew.**'

You could not do away with God's people Israel. If you did, you would have to do away with God.

This is the reason why it is being brought forth in every generation and David looked up and saw in the last days what was going to take place and said:

> **Psalm 68: 31** 'Princes shall come out of Egypt; **Ethiopia shall soon stretch out her hands unto God.**'

What God is Ethiopia going to stretch out her hand to?

> **Jeremiah 31:1** 'At the same time, saith the Lord, **will I be the God of all the families of Israel**, and **they shall be my people**.'

He said you are going to be His people, and you're not going to have to go all over the world looking for a man to come:

> **Jeremiah 23:6-7** 'In his days Judah shall be saved, and Israel shall dwell safely: and this is his name whereby he shall be called, the LORD OUR RIGHTEOUSNESS. Therefore, behold, the days come, saith the Lord, that they shall no more say, The LORD liveth, which brought up the children of Israel out of the land of Egypt;'

We are in the North now, and that is the reason why this church has got to be established in the top of the mountain. And John when he looked and seen:

> **Revelation 7:3-5a** 'Saying, **Hurt not the earth, neither the sea, nor the trees, till we have sealed the servants of our God in their foreheads.** And I heard the number of them which were sealed: and **there were sealed an hundred and forty and four thousand of all the tribes of the children of Israel**. Of the tribe of Juda were sealed twelve thousand.'

If it is a gentile tribe or whatever, come on in and allow yourself, your heart to be circumcised by the Spirit of

God and wear the name that God called you, because there isn't but one mother and one father. And it says:

> **Ephesians 4:6** 'One God and Father of all, who is above all, and through all, **and in you all.**'

And if you got this God in you, listen to what God said:

> **Psalm 33:12 'Blessed is the nation whose God is the Lord;'**

Then what you ought to want to know is who is the Lord?

> **Exodus 15:3 'The Lord is a man of war**: the Lord is his name.'

The Lord is a man and:

> **Isaiah 7:20 'In the same day shall the Lord shave with a razor.'**

It must be a man if he is shaving.

> **Psalm 33:12 'Blessed is the nation whose God is the Lord**; and the people whom he hath chosen for his own inheritance.'

Who did he choose when once they were to be destroyed, and he said:

> **Jeremiah 12:10 'Many pastors have destroyed my vineyard**, they have trodden **my portion under foot**, they have made **my pleasant portion** a desolate wilderness.'

1) God what is your **vineyard**?

> **Isaiah 5:7 'For the vineyard of the Lord of hosts is the house of Israel**, and the men of Judah his pleasant plant: and he looked for judgment, but behold oppression; for righteousness, but behold a cry.'

2) God who is your **portion**?

Deuteronomy 32:9 'For the Lord's **portion is his people**; Jacob is the lot of his inheritance.'

3) God who is your **people**?

Matthew 2:6 'And thou Bethlehem, in the land of Juda, art not the least among the princes of Juda: for out of thee shall come a Governor, **that shall rule my people Israel.**'

4) God who is **Israel**?

Amos 9:7 'Are ye not as children of the Ethiopians" [Notice God didn't say any of these: niggers, jigaboos, negroes, spooks, darkies, colored people]

'**unto me, O children of Israel?** saith the Lord. Have not I brought up Israel out of the land of Egypt?' No. God said you are of the Ethiopians to me and your Spiritual name is Israel.

The reason you can't become to be a nation and have your right up under the sun is because you are wearing another name and not the name that God gave you.

And I *(King of Israel, italics mine)* have come after you! My object is to build a city for you to go up to where you can have your identity. You are never going to have your rights up under the sun, and you don't have nothing to represent under the state. In the United States, you must have something to represent. That is the reason why John said in Revelation:

Revelation 21:1-2a 'And I saw a new heaven and a new earth: for the first heaven and the first earth were passed away; and there was no more sea. And I John saw the holy city, new

> Jerusalem, **coming down from God out of heaven....**'

What do you mean? It was coming out of a man. What is new Jerusalem? Listen, let me tell you what new Jerusalem is:

> **Ezra 1:2** 'Thus saith Cyrus king of Persia, The Lord God of heaven hath given me all the kingdoms of the earth; and **he hath charged me to build him an house at Jerusalem,** which is in Judah. 3 Who is there among you of all his people? his God be with him, and let him go up to Jerusalem, which is in Judah, and **build the house of the Lord God of Israel, (he is the God,) which is in Jerusalem.**'

That is why Joel picked it up and said:

> **Joel 2:27** 'And **ye shall know that I am in the midst of Israel**, and that **I am the Lord your God**, and none else: and **my people shall never be ashamed.**'

That's why John said:

> **Revelation 21:1** 'And I saw a new heaven and a new earth: for the first heaven and the first earth were passed away; and there was no more sea. 2 And I John saw the holy city, new Jerusalem, **coming down from God out of heaven,**'

[out of the mouth of a man]

> 'prepared as a bride adorned for her husband. 3 **And I heard a great voice out of heaven saying,**'

[And I heard a great voice out of ME saying]

> 'Behold, the tabernacle of God is with men, and he will dwell with them,'

[And I am not thinking about dying and going nowhere. I'm going to be here with you]
> 'and they shall be his people, and God himself shall be with them, and be their God."

This is the end of the sermon that was transcribed from a recording by Bishop Martin Tumpkin, the 3rd King in the organization. It was recorded on an LP before I joined The Spiritual Israel Church & Its Army. It has been reported by many who sat under his reign that before he died he used to pinch his flesh and say **that what you are looking at is God.**

TEACHING ONE THING, BUT DOES SOMETHING ELSE:

In Israel it was taught that if you served the God of Israel, you would never die referencing what Jesus said in:

> **John 8:51** "Verily, verily, I say unto you, If a man keep my saying, **he shall never see death.**"

The ministers in Israel preached that the pastors of the world were lying to you at funerals when they say, "God loved your dead loved one as the best and called them home." God created man to live and not to die. God doesn't kill and has no pleasure in death:

> **Ezekiel 18:32 "For I have no pleasure in the death of him that dieth**, saith the Lord God: wherefore turn yourselves, and live ye."

Continuing, they'd preach: You die when you just can't help it. Nobody wants to die. The roaches got more sense than people. They'd wittingly ask, what do roaches do when you walk into a dark room and turn on the lights? They scatter because they don't want to die. The roaches run for cover.

Stylistically mocking the preachers of the world, the Israel minister would proceed:

"They tell you that when you get to heaven you are going to get your wings [and the people shout, yea - yea]. You'll get two wings on your feet, two wings on your hips, and two wings on your shoulders and you are just going to fly all over heaven praising God."

But sarcastically he'd asked the congregation:

"How many wings do it take for those little birds to fly? Two. And how many wings do those huge jets and airplanes have that fly the sky with hundreds of people? Two. But these lying pastors tell you that you're going to need six.

And they tell you, "When you get to heaven, you are going to get slippers and walk the streets paved with gold. All you are going to eat and drink is milk and honey and every day is going to be Sunday."

Using dramatics and shaking his head in disbelief, the minister would pose the questions

- "What are you going to do?
- Some of you have got corns on your feet and will holler if cotton touches them. You can't hardly wear slippers down here.
- Some of you have digestive systems that can't handle milk and honey down here, so what are you going to eat?
- Some of you don't like working down here; so who is going to clean up behind those cows that give the milk?

Heaven is in you and it doesn't have to be above the sun, moon, and stars. Israel is the church of the firstborn which is written in heaven and not in the sky. Heaven is in you and not in the sky."

When it came to insurance, the God of Israel was our insurance. If you trust God, to pay for burial insurance was to doubt Him. It would be like betting against yourself. There was no thought of what a person's family would be put through trying to bury a loved one without insurance. This was considered negative thinking, and we were taught to think positive. I bought the cake, the baking pan, and the cake spoon.

When you really want to believe something, it doesn't take much of a seed planting, and everyone else waters it with their notions of truth. Everyone is drinking water from the same.

The King and the bishops said that they didn't want people that were sick in the pulpit and preaching over the people. God is a healer, God is not sickness, and in fact God said He would take all diseases off of you and put them on them that hate you. So if you're Israel, what are you doing sick?

Deuteronomy 7:15 "And the Lord will take **away from thee all sickness**, and will put none of the evil diseases of Egypt, which thou knowest, upon thee; **but will lay them upon all them that hate thee**."

But the unthinkable started happening. Pastors and Bishops were getting sick and many died. The King of Israel got sick, but how could you keep the King from the pulpit. It is amazing how we, as people, can forget what we preached yesterday and how the rules change when it comes to us and those we love. The people have eyes to see, but they see not because it would affect what they believe. Many are too fragile to deal with reality, so they choose to ignore it.

I became aware of leaders in the church who passed and had wills, funeral arrangements, and burial insurance. I saw and became aware of things that according to Israel's doctrine should only have happened to people in the world; it was happening in Israel. One tragic event that touched everyone wiped out a family's grandparent and a mother and father of the Church. These were hard working people in the

Church, people that were loved by all, and pillars. The doctrine of Israel does not explain this when it is taught that you will live forever and that the God of Israel will keep you from all hurt, harm, and danger. Others, including my family, lost loved ones in tragedies. While this did not dampen my faith in the God of Israel, to no avail, I did begin to question the doctrine within the organization.

Bishop Sidney L. Smith was over the Israel Spiritual School of Theology (ISST); he was very well loved by the people. The other bishops used to get angry at him for stating *"this short black man is going to live in this body forever."* They would be angry at him for claiming what they were actually teaching that you could too if you served the God of Israel [Israel's Doctrine]. In other words, I began to see that they, the bishops, were teaching something that they didn't actually believe themselves. Nevertheless, in the process of time, Bishop Sidney became ill and he passed.

During my membership in Israel, there were two kings that went by way of the grave: Bishop Robert Haywood, and then Bishop Jordan C. Wiley. The best account of these momentous inconsistent events of death as it related to Israel's Doctrine was; it is not that God loved them best and called them home, but rather since heaven is in you, your dead loved ones are living in you, and as long as you live they live.

CHAPTER TWELVE
ISRAEL SPIRITUAL SCHOOL OF THEOLOGY (I.S.S. OFT.):

Believe it or not (and most will not), any church can find itself practicing things contrary to sound doctrine when *the door keepers* fall asleep on the job of Biblical discernment. Many who leave other Churches bring along baggage to the new Church. Many place their experiences on the same level as Biblical discernment: their experience is **real** to them, but they're blind to the fact that it may not be **true** (Biblical). Then there is the case where **the door keepers** are nothing more than pied pipers, and people, who are in awe of them rather than *"what does the Bible teach,"* fall prey ~ victim to the doctrine of men (sprayed with the fragrance of Christianity) rather than the doctrine of Christ (with its natural aroma of truth).

It is easy to make the statement *"I would never,"* but the truth of the matter is *"but by the grace of God, there go I."* The Biblical warnings are not written to the other fellow, but they are written to us. The major sign of error in any religious teaching, even when there is usage of Scripture, is the absence of "Jesus Christ" and the promotion of "you."

SPIRITISM: "Those who believe profess many different religions: Witchcraft, Paganism, Voodoo, and New Age ideology all teach that the dead can be reached through various means. Theosophy and Eastern religions paste a veneer of respectability over what is nothing more than the influence of demons in psychic phenomena. Now more than ever, the influence of those attempting communication with the dead pervades modern culture. People have embraced an

Eastern type of cultic Christianity, lightly sprayed with Biblical terminology."[27]

This section was added to demonstrate how an organization can develop principles and practices that the Bible clearly condemns and warns against. But either through ignorance of theology or believing that one has some insight of finding something (secret) that God has hid or kept from others, a doctrine is established claiming the Scriptures as its foundation. Sadly, the unsuspecting lost sheep follow their blind leaders down the path of the occult believing they are learning the things of God.

> **Philippians 3:8** "Yea doubtless, **and I count all things but loss** for the excellency of the knowledge of Christ Jesus my Lord: for whom I have suffered the loss of all things, **and do count them but dung**, that I may win Christ,"

> **Philippians 3:13-14** "Brethren, I count not myself to have apprehended: **but this one thing I do, forgetting those things which are behind,** and reaching forth unto those things which are before, 14 I press toward the mark for the prize of the high calling of God in Christ Jesus."

There have been many who left The Spiritual Israel Church & Its Army and who now claim to profess Jesus Christ in their new Church ministries. But a review of their credentials reveals that they proudly listed (I.S.S. of T) among them with a slight name twist. For example:

> "He holds an **Honorary Doctorate degree from the Israel Seminary School of Theology**, and has furthered his doctoral aspirations by continuing his

---

[27] Martin, Walter; Rische, Jill Martin; Rische, Kevin. (2008). *The Kingdom of the Occult* (p. 29). Thomas Nelson. Kindle Edition.

education attending The Full Gospel Christian Church Bible College and Theological Seminary, where he has received his Bachelors, Masters, and Doctoral Degrees in Theology." [28]

Joseph made it clear that it was God that provided the meaning of any dream. The unknown, as well as the known, is in God's hand.

"They said to him, 'We have had dreams, and there is no one to interpret them.' And Joseph said to them, '**Do not interpretations belong to God?** Please tell them to me.'" **Genesis 40:8** (ESV)

Joseph was not practicing or trying to master Godship. He did not offer a package on how to interpret dreams or get a diploma on dream interpretation.

The Scripture encourages and admonishes us "**to ask God,**" but there is no one who can command God (Father, Son, Holy Spirit) to do anything. God said in the Scriptures: "Thus says the Lord, the Holy One of Israel, and the one who formed him:

- **Ask me of things to come;**

- **will you command me**

    concerning my children and the work of my hands?" **Isaiah 45:11** (ESV)

God is saying, Talk to Me about it!

- **Do not talk** to the crystal balls or the bearded prophets;

- **Do not talk** to the people who read palms or tea leaves;

- **Do not talk** to the people who claim to know secret things.

---

[28] http://www.victorywordchurch.org Retrieved 05/13/2016

And then He gives His credentials: "I have made the earth, and created man on it. I—My hands—stretched out the heavens, and all their host I have commanded. I have raised him up in righteousness, and I will direct all his ways" (vv. 12–13). God ends with the promise that Israel shall be saved by God "with an everlasting salvation" (v. 17).'[29]

The I.S.S. of T. manual states that the school was founded by the "*True and Living God*." It claims that:

> "there is no teaching in any school, or from any source, that can compare or compete with the teaching in this school, for its source is from the highest, and all his precepts are truth."

Only members of The Spiritual Israel Church & Its Army, and who are in good standing are allowed to pursue **I.S.S.** of T. classes. All teachers and instructors must be approved by the president of **I.S.S. of T. and the King of Israel.**

> A student of **I.S.S. of T.** was required to complete 33 lessons (33 Degrees) to graduate with the confirmed title of *doctor or madam* from Israel's school of theology within a year (Israel's year was from June to June). Graduating students received the Certificate and card during the General Assembly held each June. If a student failed or dropped out of the class, they were allowed to repeat it as many times as necessary until they demonstrated that they had mastered all 33 *Lessons*. Each lesson is a degree. Thirty-three degrees denotes a master. Israel did not believe in practicing what it called 'Black Art.'"

According to the manual (**I.S.S. of T.**):

---

[29] Martin, Walter; Rische, Jill Martin; Rische, Kevin (2008-10-21). The Kingdom of the Occult (p. 60). Thomas Nelson. Kindle Edition.

"All teachings and instructions, must be according to this book **(I.S.S. of T.)**. There will be no black art, voodoo, or any such thing taught with or in these classes. All this is witchcraft and is a work of the flesh as recorded in Galatians 5:19-21."

But the **(I.S.S. of T.)** manual teachings clearly violates God's Word, as you will see, coming out of the gate. You will also find teachings related to Mystics, Word of Faith, and FreeMasonry to name a few.

Each Lesson has Scriptures associated with the practice. The Instructor evaluates the student's demonstration of the lessons as each class moves forward.

Elements Of Moses Scriptures	
Air	Exodus 10:19
Darkness	Exodus 10:21 - 23
Earth	Exodus 15:12
Fire	Exodus 13: 21 - 22
Water	Exodus 14:28

Lesson 1: The Foundation of Spiritual Israel

The student was to practice coming out of self (**Affirm**) with the desire of **the Spirit telling me something**. Focus was **center**ed on the higher properties of earth, and **daily meditation** using the 23rd Psalm and the Lord's Prayer.

- **Motto:** Always do good. Wise as the serpent, bold as a lion, meek as a lamb, and harmless as a dove.
- **Byword**: (1 Kings 18:36-37). Snap of finger means dismiss foundation.
- **Black Art** is the study of the dead.

- **White Art** is the study of the higher things of the living.
- **Witness of Foundation:** The byword and motto.
- **Method of Healing:** Shadow looking on, and touch (Acts 3:4; 2 Timothy 2:5).

Associated Scripture is 1 Corinthians 12.

My Refute of Lesson 1: First, this lesson (and others) is unbiblical. Second there is no focus on Jesus Christ who is the mediator between God and man (1 Timothy 2:5). Jesus said without Him we can do nothing (John 15:5).

Lesson 2: "24 and 2" Spiritual Foundation

The student was to choose their "**Wall of Protection**" which consisted of:

a. 2 (**dead**) forces from the psychic plane. Picturing the (dead) man on your right and the (dead) woman on your left. A man and woman who has passed on, but you can remember them as they were while they lived. Do not use those that were against you.

b. The 24 forces were made up of **the living** (12 men on your right and 12 women on your left). These must be Israelites. They should be at least 12 years of age. Others outside of Israel should be used only in your legion of angels. Legion is many. Angels are those that are sent by God to do a certain work or carry a message; spiritually or naturally so. Matthew 26:53.

The student had to write the Wall of Protection forces (12 men/12 women) on two small sheets of paper, and in the case of death, replace the name(s) appropriately. Associated Scriptures are Romans 12, Job 19:8, Lamentation 3:7, Luke 16:26-29, Deuteronomy 32:38-39.

My Refute of Lesson 2: Saul got in trouble for communicating with the dead: 1 Samuel 28:3-19; 1 Chronicles 10:13-14. The Bible forbids the practice of mediums and necromancers; (Leviticus 19:31).

Lesson 3: Your Main Spiritual Guide

The student:

a. Call up their **Wall of Protections**.

b. Call up their **24 forces**.

c. Concentrate on t**he King of Israel** (the man who is over the organization). He is the **main Spiritual Guide**: Ask your positive and negative forces to operate through the King of Israel (the Spiritual Guide). The student is their own negative force, and the King is their positive force. He is your main spiritual guide; the power which is the supreme God, that dwells supreme in the positive force. **Only through your positive force can you contact the Supreme God**. Use these words: I am calling for the power of the spirit of (whatever or whoever you are calling for) to come into my vibrations.

Associated Scriptures are Matthew; John 16:13.

My Refute of Lesson 3: Jesus Christ is the mediator between God and man (1 Timothy 2:5). Jesus said without Him we can do nothing (John 15:5). The leader of the organization is not the "**Spirit of Truth**" that Jesus promised.

Lesson 4: The Power of The Spiritual Glass of Water

The student calls up their **Wall of Protection/forces and Guide**. This lesson is used:

a. **For changing conditions:** Set a glass of water in the room, let it stand for three or seven days. Throw it outside on the ground (dirt).

b. **For those that can't sleep or poor memory; also those who can't have clear dreams or can't sleep:** Set a glass of water under the bed for 3 days and 3 nights.

c. To Master conditions, use the elements of Moses.

d. **Additions: Place a glass of water in the palm of your left hand, read Psalm 34, and drink the water after reading.** Do this five nights straight.

Associated Scriptures Genesis 1, Job 22:6-7, Exodus 15:27, Matthew 3:8.

My Refute of Lesson 4: This lesson is unbiblical and has no Biblical precedence.

Lesson 5: Spiritual Readings and The Way to Give Them

The student calls up their **Wall of Protection/forces and Guide**. To read spiritually is to come out of your thoughts, and not be influenced by your five senses. This is how the spirit may contact you from inside or outside of you. The spirit leads us through the heart, soul, and mind.

- Clairvoyance is the ability to hear spiritually.
- Psychic is the ability to see spiritually.
- To pick-up is the ability to feel spiritually.

This is all done from within you. Your only physical sense that works both natural and spiritual is your feelings. Your body has your physical feelings; your soul has your inner feelings. To read always use Colossians 4:3-6 and be sure to follow its instructions. The purpose of reading is to advise, warn, bless, or help someone; never to upset, scare, debase, or get anyone into any kind of trouble.

The student:

a. When **Reading a Person**, look or center your gaze between their eyes.
   - If addressing a man, use the word "**Sir**."
   - If addressing a lady, use the word "**Madam**."

b. Memorize Colossians 4:3- 6; John 4:16.

c. Begin muscular **reading** until you pick up the **spiritual forces**. If the person is "**ill**" or "**well**" looking, make the statement.

d. People who have narrow eyes & narrow mouth are classed for deceit.

e. Mouth held slightly open is an honest mouth.

f. Thin eyebrows is quick tempered.

g. Big or large eyes talks a lot.

h. Nose that stands out and is round, is stubborn and likes to have their way.

i. Thin lips are good speakers and good teachers.

j. High forehead carries good thoughts and makes good companions.

k. Broad forehead reasons out good ideas and has good ideas.

l. Narrow forehead is an untruthful and hard to get along with.

Associated Scripture is 2 Kings 5:15-27.

My Refute of Lesson 5: There is no Biblical precedence for this lesson. We can't determine a person's integrity by trying to read their outward appearance John 7:24.

Lesson 6: How to Pray in The Spirit

The student calls up their **Wall of Protection/forces and Guide**.

a. The student is to ask the Holy Father for what is needed and what is wanted.

b. Meet the spiritual forces at least four times a day

Angels: Michael morning, **Uriel** noon, **Raphael** evening, Gabriel midnight.

c. Prayer is the key to the kingdom, but faith unlocks the door. Read in the turning point book of the Bible (Psalm 23).

d. Scriptures used to help one gain faith: Exodus 15:1-21; Deuteronomy 32:1-44; Hebrews 11; Matthew 6:1-15; John 11:41-42; 2 Kings 20:1-4; 1 Kings 8:22.

Associated Scripture is Psalm 121.

My Refute of Lesson 6: This lesson uses nonbiblical angels from the apocrypha. The apocryphal books are not inspired writings and are not included in the closed canon.

Lesson 7: How to Send Spiritual Messages

The student calls up their **Wall of Protection/forces and Guide**.

a. Place **two chairs** in the center of the floor facing each other.

b. The student sits in one chair and places the subject (spiritually) in the other chair:

  1. Drive out the **evil influences** of this subject (person),

2. And put a **good spirit** in them, and tell them what you want them to do.

c. To send a message, sit down and use spiritual paper and pencil. Write your message stating what you want that person to do. Take it to the mail box and mail it. Stamp it if it is a letter. If it is a telegram, take it to the telegraph office. Results from 3–7 days.

Associated Scripture is Matthew 8: 3-4, 22-27.

My Refute of Lesson 7: This lesson is unbiblical. The men in Scripture didn't practice channeling messages; they trusted God and in His authority. By what authority are the evil forces (demons) being driven out? Nothing about the name of Jesus is in the lesson. If the person (non-Christian) does not accept Jesus Christ, they are not delivered (Luke 11:24-26). A Christian cannot be demon possessed, because their body is the temple of God (1 Corinthians 3:16; 1 Corinthians 6:19). Possession (internal) and oppression (external) are not the same thing. Both non-Christians and Christians can be influenced (external) by oppression, but not possession.

Lesson 8: Spiritual Super-Trance and How To Do It

The student calls up their **Wall of Protection/forces and Guide**.

Super-Trance: Seeking into the universe for that which is hidden across and beyond.

- The Super-Trance is used to locate **missing persons** and **stolen articles**.
- **Speak the word** before concentrating; back it up with Isaiah 55:11 and 1 Samuel 3:19.
- Concentrate on the missing person or stolen article.

- - Close all else in your mind.
  - Be sure you are dressed with spirituals forces.
  - You may lay down or sit. Be sure to relax completely.
- The student should give themselves three to nine days to restore such.

Associated Scripture is Hebrews 4:12.

My Refute of Lesson 8: We are not little gods. We don't call things into existence; only God can do that. Jesus instructed us to ask the Father.

Lesson 9: Spiritual Double Arrow

The student calls up their **Wall of Protection/forces and Guide**.

Double Arrow: This is used for severe headaches and loss of memory. It as a two-fold work:

- Removing Pain.
- Replacing Energy.

Place (shoot) a double arrow at one glance into the thought chamber and temple.

- Picture an arrow with a double shaft as an electric cord with the positive and negative wires attached but running parallel one to the other.
- Picture an arrow point on both shafts.
- Shoot an arrow into the thought chamber, having it split as it goes between the eyes.
- Picture the positive shaft going to the right and the negative shaft going to the left.
  - Follow them up or down to the condition. Bring them back together at the condition.

- For "A Reading" after using arrow, have it return to you.
- If the student is working on self, use looking into a mirror.

Associated Scriptures 2 Samuel 22:15; Psalms 32:8, 76:3; Proverbs 25:18; Deuteronomy 32:8, 23, 34.

My Refute of Lesson 9: This lesson is unbiblical. No Biblical precedence.

Lesson 10: How To Restore One Into Their Right Mind

The student calls up their **Wall of Protection/forces and Guide**.

Restore: This is used for people who are intoxicated or insane. You may wash evil thoughts, words, deeds, etc. out of a person's heart, mind, and soul by the washing of water by the word. If one or more (heart, soul, mind) is cluttered up with an evil force, picture the word cleansing them like as with water. If the problem is more chronic, use transformation of spirit by psychic energy.

Place person before you:

- If it is a man, call one of your male forces.
- If it is a lady, call one of your female forces.

1. **Remove the** (good) **mind from a** person that can bear the cause of your client's insanity.

2. **Remove the** (insane) **mind from the** person * in front of you, and replace it with the good mind.

3. **Place the** (insane) **mind into the** person that can bear the cause of your client's insanity.

4. **Command the spirit** to stop him seven times and to hold him seven times. (Romans 12:2).

Associated Scripture is Matthew 15:22.

My Refute of Lesson 10: This lesson is totally unbiblical. And what spirit is being commanded? Surely not the Holy Spirit.

Lesson 11: Healing One at a Distance

The student calls up their **Wall of Protection/forces and Guide.**

This is used to drive out evil forces that has a person bound. If necessary, the student should operate on the person. **When healing from a distance**:

a. Lay subject stretched out on a bed.

b. If the student does not know what the person looks like, get a description of the person's features.

c. Student homework: Find out how these **men mastered these conditions by healing at a distance**: Elisha, Jacob, Jesus Christ, Paul. Compare with lessons from 2 King 4:36, Jeremiah 30:17, Isaiah 48:17, Exodus 15:26.

Associated Scripture is Hosea 13:14, Isaiah 28:14 (Power).

My Refute of Lesson 11: This lesson is unbiblical. The men in Scripture didn't practice mastering conditions, they trusted God and in His authority. Jesus Christ was fully God and fully man. By what authority are the evil forces (demons) being driven out? Nothing about in the name of Jesus is in the lesson. If the person (non-Christian) does not accept Jesus Christ, they are not delivered (Luke 11: 24-26). A Christian cannot be demon possessed, because their body is the temple of God (1 Corinthians 3:16; 1 Corinthians 6:19). What discernment was used to determine whether:

- The person was mentally ill and under a psychiatrist care and simply not taking their medication?
- Demon possessed?
- Mentally ill and demon possessed?

Lesson 12: How To Re-Unite The Separated And To Find Lost Ones

The student calls up their **Wall of Protection/forces and Guide**. If it is known that a person wants a companion back to misuse, abuse, mistreat, or any such like; It is wrong help them get them back for any reason or amount of money.

a. Take a piece of brown wrapping paper and make a square.

b. Write the names of **the persons to be re-united on it**. If you have not seen the persons(s), get a description.

d. Draw a continuous line around each letter of the names.

e. Fold holding your desire.

f. Make a mixture of 1 teaspoon of Alum or Honey, 1 tablespoon of Vinegar, 1 teaspoon of Red pepper. Mix and shake well in a bottle of water. Set aside.

Associated Scriptures Proverbs 12, Psalm 69:21, Lamentation 3:19, Matthew 27:34, Mark 15:36, Luke 23:26, John 19:29, Exodus 24:4.

My Refute of Lesson 12: This lesson is unbiblical. God gave man free will, even He does not force any man or woman to reconcile with Him.

Lesson 13: Cleansing Your World and The World of Others

The student calls up their **Wall of Protection/forces and Guide.**

a. Place pan of water in center of floor.

b. Cut an apple or potato into four pieces and place them in the pan of water.

c. Call upon the spirit forces of the four winds and place them in the pan.

d. Visualize yourself or (client) in the center of the apple or potato, then state your complaint.

e. Call upon the God of Abraham, Isaac, and Israel, scattering with the four winds.

f. Go out into the open field or yard, and throw each piece (in the pan) in each direction: East, West, South, North.

Associated Scriptures Romans 15, Psalm 19:12, Proverbs 20:30.

My Refute of Lesson 13: This lesson is unbiblical. It is God's Word that cleanses us. It is Jesus Christ that washes us Revelation1:5; Ephesians 5:26; and 1 Corinthians 6:11. **1John 1:9 "If we confess our sins**, he is faithful and just to forgive us our sins, and **to cleanse us from all unrighteousness."** No one can confess for you. No mixing of a concoction will ever replace being washed in the blood of Christ.

Lesson 14: Changing Your Own or Someone Else's Life Forever

The student calls up their **Wall of Protection/forces and Guide**.

    a. Call the subject who needs change before you.

    b. Set two chairs facing each other.

- Sit in one chair, and place the subject in the other chair.
- If it is yourself needing change, place yourself spiritually in the other chair.

    c. **Remove the evil spirit and place the evil spirit into a stone.** Then put **a good spirit** in the place of **the evil spirit**. You may do this by the transformation of spirit or by reprogramming the person's heart, mind, and soul with words of the utmost strength in truth against the spirit of trouble that has the person bound.

    d. Take it to the river and drop it in, repeating these words three times: **I have changed your life forever**.

Associated Scripture is Mark 5: 2-13.

My Refute of Lesson 14: This lesson is unbiblical. We do good if we change our own lives, through coming to Christ (2 Corinthians 5:17-18; Galatians 6:15-17). The men in Scripture didn't practice mastering conditions or changing others, they preached the gospel in the authority given by God. By what authority are the evil spirts (demons) being removed? If the Holy Ghost is not the one with whom they are being filled, they are still in trouble. Nothing about in the name of Jesus is in the lesson. If the person (non-Christian) does not accept Jesus Christ, they are not delivered (Luke 11: 24-26). A Christian cannot be demon possessed because their body is the temple of God (1 Corinthians 3:16; 1 Corinthians 6:19). What discernment was used to determine whether:

- the person was mentally ill, under a psychiatrist care, and simply not taking their medication?
- demon possessed?
- or mentally ill and demon possessed?

Lesson 15: Money and Spiritual Ways to Get It

The student calls up their **Wall of Protection/forces and Guide**. Money is the answer to all things. The power of money is the ability to achieve the things you desire in righteousness, without money.

Ask the spirit for the power of money, and after receiving it, do as the spirit demands.

- There are three means of obtaining it: playing, debt, and finding it.
- When contributing, make the contribution to 12 tribes.
- There is power in song of Moses, Deuteronomy 32:44. And the song of David in 2 Samuel 22.

Associated Scriptures Acts 5:1-14, Matthew 2:11; 2 Kings 5:26, Ecclesiastes 7:12, Isaiah 52:3, Matthew 17:24, Matthew 22:19, Matthew 25:18, Luke 9:3, Mark 6:8, 1 Timothy 6:10.

My Refute of Lesson 15: This lesson is unbiblical. 1 John 5:14. Matthew 6: 31-34.

Proverbs 30:7-9 "Two things have I required of thee; deny me them not before I die: Remove far from me vanity and lies: give me neither poverty nor riches; feed me with food convenient for me: Lest I be full, and deny thee, and say, Who is the Lord? or lest I be poor, and steal, and take the name of my God in vain."

Lesson 16: How to Make What You Say Take

The student calls up their **Wall of Protection/forces and Guide**.

This is used for approaching people or asking favors.

Ask the spirit to let what you say take, then ask the Father to grant you the words of deliverance. Ask three times.

This is for approaching people or asking favors likewise.

Associated Scriptures John 1:1-14, Acts 25:21.

My Refute of Lesson 16: This lesson is unbiblical. If you are "asking," you are not making. What you ask may not be in accord with the will of God. When asking God, the reply can also be "No." If God says no, it does not matter what you say. Genesis 17:18-19 (No to Abraham); Deuteronomy 3:25-26 (No to Moses); 2 Corinthians 12:8-10 (No to Paul).

Lesson 17: How to Use Natural Medicine Spiritually

The student calls up their **Wall of Protection/forces and Guide**.

   a. Visualize yourself going to the drugstore, and then returning and preparing the medicine.

   b. Give it to the person, then drive it down their throat using the spiritual "**double arrow**," with forces behind them.

   c. If there is any medicine on hand that you want to take, bless the medicine before taking it. Use Psalm 6 over it.

Associated Scripture is Psalm 6.

My Refute of Lesson 17: Pray, read, and then follow the doctor's instructions.

Lesson 18: How to Heal Yourself

The student calls up their **Wall of Protection/forces and Guide**.

a. Use mirror or chair, shoot a spiritual "**double arrow**" into the mind force.

b. Follow the "**double arrow**" down or up to the condition.

c. Then ask the spirit for deliverance.

If necessary, use a spiritual glass of water.

- **Rebuke spirit that has the body bound.**
- Have patience and tarry.

Pray - Holy Father, grant me peace, joy, health, happiness and success; in my home, also at the end eternal life.

Associated Scriptures John 15: 3,7, & 11, 14:1-2 Psalm 107:20; Psalm 6 and 121.

My Refute of Lesson 18: This lesson is unbiblical. What spirit is being rebuked? See refute notes on lesson 11 and 14.

Lesson 19: How to Forget Past Mistakes

The student calls up their **Wall of Protection/forces and Guide**. Make certain that the client forgives all who they may have something against, regardless of how much they feel they have a right to hold it against any, then you may proceed.

a. Get a piece of brown wrapping paper, and write the client's complaint in the center, ask the client if that is all.

b. Fold the paper as small as possible:
- Place it in a saucer.
- Set it on fire.

c. After the client leaves, take the ashes that remain:
- Carry the ashes to a window and **command the spirit of the four winds** to carry these mistakes away.
- Give the client a commandment connected with lesson #10.

  Associated Scriptures Acts 17:20-23, Psalm 121.

My Refute of Lesson 19: This lesson is unbiblical. No Biblical precedence.

Lesson 20: How to Cause Yourself or Anyone Else to Rest in Peace

The student calls up their **Wall of Protection/forces and Guide.** Make certain that you or the client forgives all who you may have ought against also repent for any evil that continually harasses your mind, then you may proceed.

a. Get a square piece of brown paper, and write the name of the person and the condition on it:
- Put a circle around it, and fold the paper.
- Then place the paper in your pocket or where it can be touched.

b. Each time you touch it, ask the spirit to give deliverance and to let it be made manifest for your name's sake.

Note: Give the client a piece of brown paper. Let the client write their complaint on it. Place it in their hand and hold it over a glass of water while reading Psalm 121.

My Refute of Lesson 20: This lesson is unbiblical. No Biblical precedence.

Lesson 21: How to Turn Enemies or Anyone Else to Friends

The student calls up their **Wall of Protection/forces and Guide**. Forgive the person first, by making certain you have nothing against them, then go on with lesson.

   a. Call the person you have in mind as an enemy **to you spiritually**.
   b. Place them in a chair and **rebuke the force of the enemy**.
   c. Then place in them the mind **you desire them to have.**
   d. Ask the Holy Father to tell you **why the person is an enemy to you**.
   e. Then, when you know why, **approach that person with the statement spiritually**.
   f. Give them the commandment of peace seven times.
   g. Write their name on a brown piece of paper, carry it with you, and talk to them.

Associated Scripture is Psalm 37.

My Refute of Lesson 21: This lesson is unbiblical. No Biblical precedence.

Lesson 22: Changing One's Will or Desire

The student calls up their **Wall of Protection/forces and Guide**. Make certain that you or the person is willing to change.

   a. **For mastering every desire**, the word of **power** is God.

   b. Changing one's condition of natural habits **from a bad habit form** to a good one.

   c. Get a piece of brown paper, and give it to the client.

   d. Let the client write the condition on it, ask the client if that is all.

   - Place the paper in a saucer.
   - Set it on fire, burning it in front of the client. Give the client a commandment.
   - After the client leaves, place the client (spiritually) in a chair before you.
   - **Remove the client's mind** and give them the mind of an outside force that is responsible. Give a commandment of peace three times. Note: find use for the Word of God.

   Associated Scriptures Romans 12:1-3, 23; 1 Samuel 3:19.

My Refute of Lesson 22: This lesson is unbiblical. No Biblical precedence.

Lesson 23: Stopping the Mouths of Lions

The student calls up their **Wall of Protection/forces and Guide**.

   a. This lesson is used for anyone having a higher position or more power than you such as lawyers, doctors, police, or anyone having power over you.

b. **Ask the Holy Father through the guide** (King of Israel) to hold control over this person that I might receive my desire.

c. Use prayer by the spirit.

d. For court cases, read Psalm 5, 6, and 8 three times.

Associated Scriptures Acts 26:28-31. Find out how these men did it: Paul and John the Revelator.

My Refute of Lesson 23: This lesson is unbiblical. No Biblical precedence.

Lesson 24: How to Make the Clouds and Rain Obey Your Will

The student calls up their **Wall of Protection/forces and Guide**.

a. This lesson is good for weather storms, storms at sea, and storms of confusion.

b. Call for **the power of the Rain God** when you are caught in a cloud or rain.

c. Call for **the power of the spirit of the rain God**. Look up, shoot your forces into the cloud with your spiritual double arrow. Call upon the **supreme God**, asking him to split the cloud and hold the rain until you reach shelter safely.

d. If you have a trip to make and you are afraid the weather will be bad, ask the Holy Father to hold back the clouds, stopping the rain or snow.

e. If you cannot memorize Joshua 10:13-14, then think upon a scripture two-fold; one to withhold and one for rain.

Associated Scripture is Matthew 8:23-28. Search Scriptures for those with rain.

My Refute of Lesson 24: This lesson is unbiblical. No Biblical precedence. Plus, this lesson references more than one God. Biblical Israelites did not worship a rain God; this is paganism.

Lesson 25: How to Make Running Water Obey Your Will

The student calls up their **Wall of Protection/forces and Guide**.

a. The place you desire to be dammed up or boxed, set your dam or box there. Hedge it up with a concrete wall (spiritually).

b. Then ask for the elements of Moses: sealing with your forces and guide and the help of the four winds on the four sides.

c. Give a commandment to the wind **seven times in each direction**. Mostly used for fishing.

d. You may do the same for people whose mouths run like water. That is if they are causing confusion and preying on the weak.

Associated Scripture is Luke 8:24.

My Refute of Lesson 25: This lesson is unbiblical. No Biblical precedence.

Lesson 26: Break-Down and Kick Back

The student calls up their **Wall of Protection/forces and Guide**.

If a sudden attack is made upon you, **vibrate a message** by spiritual telephone or telegram for a double breakdown, and **it should kick back at the enemy**.

Associated Scripture is Matthew 26:50-53.

My Refute of Lesson 26: This lesson is unbiblical. No Biblical precedence.

Lesson 27: Splitting the Planet

The student calls up their **Wall of Protection/forces and Guide.** Splitting the planet is the ability to go beyond the physical world of a person, and enter the spirit world, and call them back to their physical form. To do so, sometimes we must use transformation of the spirit by using psychic energy to give them a spirit until they return. If their SIN is not too great, they will return. The body must also be strong enough to retain or hold the spirit after they return.

a. In case **someone is ill and physicians have given up:**
   - Dismiss all from the room.
   - Use the Scripture 2 Kings 4:30-37, and call for your guide (King of Israel).
   - Note: if possible, use adjustments.

b. If person has not the **mind or hope** use lesson #10.
   - If necessary to operate, do so.
   - If you can't reach your desired force with the ill person, use **transformation of the spirit**.
   - If necessary, use **psychic energy**.
   - Use prayer by faith.

c. Renew the fight and continue to fight after you see improvement.

Associated Scripture is Isaiah 38:1-5.

My Refute of Lesson 27: This lesson is unbiblical. No Biblical precedence.

Lesson 28: How to Be Fearless and Lion Like

The student calls up their **Wall of Protection/forces and Guide**.

- Be sharp as an arrow, harmless as a dove, strong as a lion, and wise as a serpent.
- Place your forces forward to accomplish any great task that you have before you.
- For court cases, shoot a spiritual double arrow into the corner of the mouth of opponent:
  - ask forces for lock and to lock.
  - if you are absent, draw a mental picture of court room with judges, etc.
  - do this before court session. Go before court opens and use a lock.

  Note: Step in with right foot first. Connect with lesson 12.

  Associated Scriptures 1 Peter 5:8, Daniel 6:11-down.

My Refute of Lesson 28: This lesson is unbiblical. No Biblical precedence.

Lesson 29: Rolling the Stone Away

The student calls up their **Wall of Protection/forces and Guide**.

a. Place stone or picture of one before you.

b. Cut a door inside the stone.

c. Place all mistakes, disheartening(s), discomforts, disease, etc. within the stone and close the door.

d. Roll stone away from you to the river and let the stone sink.

e. Repeat these words: "With this stone I have rolled your troubles away."

Associated Scripture is Isaiah 58.

My Refute of Lesson 29: This lesson is unbiblical. No Biblical precedence.

Lesson 30: The Spiritual Fee System

Tuition: $35.00 is to be paid during the first week of the General Assembly.

Monthly Payments: $15.00 to be paid during the first class of each month for the first eight months.

- The student fee will then be paid in full.
- There will be no charge for cases or work.
- After student graduates and receives a diploma, **they may set a fee for cases or work**.
- All fees will be announced as donations.

Lesson 31: The Password, Grip, Secret Knock, And Distress Signal

a. **Password:** Spiritual Israel

b. **Grip:** Clinch little fingers, slide thumb back and forth on first three knuckles.

c. **Secret Knock:** Give two knocks and rattle with back of fingers.

d. **Distress Signal:** Right hand to heart, stomach, sliding to side.

My Refute of Lesson 31: This lesson is unbiblical. No Biblical precedence.

Lesson 32: Interpretation of Dreams

The student calls up their **Wall of Protection/forces and Guide**.

a. If mind is not clear, concentrate into a spiritual glass of water.

b. After your mind is clear, hold (focus) your mind on your guide (King of Israel).

c. Then, ask the God of Abraham, Isaac, and Israel (Jacob) [Which is faith (heart); and Obedience (soul) which is feeling; Overcoming five senses (mind)] to reveal the interpretation of the secret of the dream to you. Repeat Amos 3:7.

d. Used for game of chance (lottery, etc.). This is your numerical guide for interpretation of dreams. If the spirit gives you anything to go along with this interpretation, use it accordingly.

A	B	C	D	E	F	G	H	I	J
K	L	M	N	O	P	Q	R	S	T
U	V	W	X	Y	Z				
1	2	3	4	5	6	7	8	9	0

My Refute of Lesson 32: This lesson is unbiblical. No Biblical precedence. Numerology New Agers mimic the occult with numerology by affixing values and meanings to certain numbers in order to interpret them as meaningful signs for past or future events. Pythagoras (c. 550 BC) and his followers added their numerology to the zodiac system in the quest for precise forecasts.[30]

It is not necessary to see a psychiatrist or a psychologist or to dabble in dream analysis to find out the meaning of dreams. Genesis 40:8 says, "Do not interpretations [of dreams] belong to God?" The answer is yes, they do. God holds the key to all interpretation. The word interpret in Hebrew is pathar, which means "to **open up**." Do not inquire of the wizards or the mediums; ask the Lord for direct information. "And when they say to you, 'Seek those who are mediums and wizards, who whisper and mutter,' should not a people seek their God? Should they seek the dead on behalf of the living?" (Isaiah 8:19-20). God is the one who will provide information, and He is willing (up to a point) to give people that assurance.[31]

Lesson 33: The End Of All Things – Rock Bottom

    a. At this point there is nothing impossible.

    b. All doubts are put to an end.

    c. That which is said cannot be done, **it will be done**.

> These 33 lessons are used to manifest The God of Israel's name, teaching, doctrine, truth, and word by the spirit. Let God be true and all men liars. Ye shall know the truth, and the truth shall make you free.

My Refute of Lesson 33: This lesson is unbiblical. No Biblical precedence. The Bible does not bear witness to even one of the 33 degrees (lessons). There is NAME missing,

---

[30] Martin, Walter; Rische, Jill Martin; Rische, Kevin (2008). The Kingdom of the Occult (p.197, 278). Thomas Nelson. Kindle Edition.

[31] Martin, Walter; Rische, Jill Martin; Rische, Kevin (2008). The Kingdom of the Occult (p. 264). Thomas Nelson. Kindle Edition.

Jesus, and the teachings are also unauthorized. They are the teachings of man. Notice these Biblical passages below (*bullet points and parenthesis are mine*).

Luke 10:17 And the seventy returned again with joy, saying, Lord, **even the devils are subject unto us through thy name**.

Act 19:13-20 Then certain of the vagabond Jews, exorcists,

- took upon them to call over them which had evil spirits the name of the Lord Jesus, saying, **We adjure you by Jesus** whom Paul preacheth. 14 And there were seven sons of one Sceva, a Jew, and chief of the priests, which did so. 15
- **And the evil spirit answered and said**, Jesus I know, and Paul I know; but who are ye?
- And **the man in whom the evil spirit was** leaped on them, and overcame them, and prevailed against them, so that they fled out of that house naked and wounded. And this was known to all the Jews and Greeks also dwelling at Ephesus;
- and fear fell on them all,
- and **the name of the Lord Jesus was magnified**.
- And **many that believed** came, and **confessed**, and shewed their deeds.
- Many of them also **which used curious arts brought their books** together, and **burned them** before all men: and they counted the price of them, and found it fifty thousand pieces of silver. So mightily grew the word of God and prevailed.

Act 16:16-21 And it came to pass, as we went to prayer,

- a certain damsel possessed with **a spirit of divination *(Deuteronomy 18: 9-14)*** met us, which brought her masters much gain **by soothsaying *(Deuteronomy 18:9-14; Daniel 2:27-28)***:
- The same followed Paul and us, and cried, saying, **These men are the servants of the most high God, which shew unto us the (A) way of salvation.** And this did she many days.
- But Paul, being grieved, turned and said to the spirit, **I command thee in the name of Jesus Christ to come out of her**. And he came out the same hour.
- And when her masters saw that the hope of their gains was gone, they caught Paul and Silas, and drew them into the marketplace unto the rulers, And brought them to the magistrates, saying, These men, being Jews, do exceedingly trouble our city, **And teach customs, which are not lawful for us to receive**, neither to observe, being Romans.

The basic problem, although there are many, with those lessons is that The Spiritual Israel Church & Its Army taught that Jesus had finished His work (citing John 17:4) and was not doing anything else.

John 17:4 "I have glorified thee on the earth: **I have finished the work** which thou gavest me to do."

That is why they did not use His name, but rather inserted the King of Israel which is the man over the organization in this day and time, according to Israel's doctrine.

PSYCHIC PHENOMENA[32]

These lessons attempted to use the Bible against itself by using Scriptures out of context, as if the Scripture authorizes dabbling into these teachings of the occult (darkside), when they do not.

- Satan is the power behind occult psychic phenomena; their purpose is to deceive mankind and **lead people away from God**.
- Biblical texts, **taken out of context**, are often used to justify psychic events.
  - **Astral projection:** Astral projection refers to the ability to leave the physical body at will, in order to explore the planes found on the astral level. Astral projection is sometimes described as a controlled out of body experience.
  - **Clairaudience:** Clairaudience is the ability to receive psychic information through hearing. Many online psychics possess this ability.
  - **Clairsentience:** This is the ability to receive psychic information through sensing alone. Clairsentience differs to empathy in that any kind of information may be sensed, not just information that relates to the emotional state of a person.
  - **Clairvoyance:** Clairvoyance is the ability to receive psychic information by **seeing it in the mind's eye**. Many psychics describe clairvoyance as similar to watching a film play in their mind.

---

[32] http://www.exploringpsychics.com/articles/psychics/types-psychic-phenomena

- **Empathy:** An empath is **a person who feels other people's emotions psychically.** Empaths feel the emotions of other people acutely, and sometimes pick up health issues or the state of mind of the people around them.

- **Lucid dreaming:** Lucid dreaming refers to **the ability to control our dreams** as we sleep. Many psychics practice lucid dreaming, to help them to gain more control over their mind and enhance their psychic abilities.

- **Precognition: Precognition is the ability to know the future.** When you have an online psychic reading, your reader is more than likely to use precognition at some point during the reading.

- **Psychokinesis:** Sometimes referred to as telekinesis, psychokinesis is the ability to move or alter objects using the power of the mind.

- **Psychometry:** Psychometry refers to the ability to be able to pick up psychic information by holding an object. **Some psychics use this technique to read for people**; they may hold a ring or watch that belongs to the person that wants the reading, so that they can tune in to that person psychically.

- **Telepathy:** This is the ability to communicate with others (people and animals) without speaking or even being in the same place as them. Telepathy works when psychically **charged thoughts, feelings, or information is sent to another using the power of the mind.**

There is no scriptural meaning for the term **psychic phenomena**. The psychic practitioners of Paranormal Phenomena cannot point to any relation in the Bible, it does not exist.

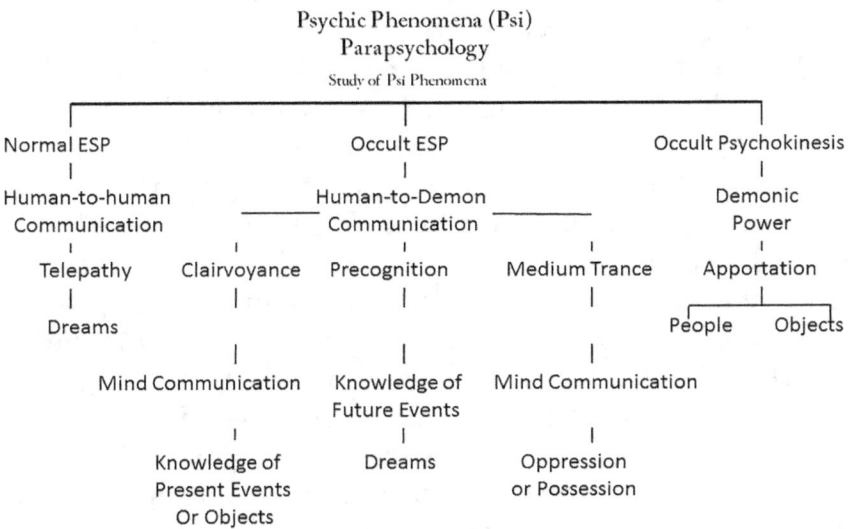

'The world of the occult is to be avoided by believers in Christ because we are the temples of the Holy Spirit (1 Corinthians 6:19).

- We are to avoid participation in the activities of this dark dimension while, at the same time, standing firmly against it to **"contend earnestly for the faith which was once for all delivered to the saints"** (Jude 3b). NKJV

- ☐ Christians are urged to put on the full armor of God to do warfare in the spiritual dimension, **confident that if we resist the devil, he will flee.**

- Remember, "He who is in you is greater than he who is in the world" (1 John 4:4b), a reference to the strength of God's power against Satan and all his hosts, **whether spiritual or corporeal"** (Ephesians 6:11; James 4:7 NKJV).'[33]

According to Walter Martin, "The world of the occult is built upon one word: **experience**. It is not built upon revealed authority. Therefore, the Christian must test all experience by divine authority. The purpose of this book is not to tear people apart or to attack them. The Bible instructs Christians to "**test everything; hold fast [cleave tenaciously] to what is good**" (1 Thessalonians 5:21 NRSV). The apostle Paul reminds us to "test everything" no matter what it appears to be. In Acts 16 and 17, he gave the glorious truth of the gospel to the Bereans, and after they heard the gospel of Christ—the Charisma, the message of redemption—they took the revelation of God Himself, examined Old Testament Scriptures, and compared what Paul said with what the Scriptures said. When they saw that it was in perfect accord, then they believed the gospel. The Scripture says they were nobler than those at Thessalonica because they searched the Scriptures (Acts 17:11)."[34]

---

[33] Martin, Walter; Rische, Jill Martin; Rische, Kevin (2008). The Kingdom of the Occult (pp. 14-15). Thomas Nelson. Kindle Edition.

[34] Martin, Walter; Rische, Jill Martin; Rische, Kevin (2008). The Kingdom of the Occult (p. 41). Thomas Nelson. Kindle Edition.

CHAPTER THIRTEEN
OTHER GROUPS: HEBREW ~ ISRAEL ~ JEWS

QUICK TIPS FOR MEETING WITH BLACK HEBREW ISRAELITES

There are no quick tips for meeting with the Black Hebrew Israelites or any other false religions. If you don't know your Bible, don't do it. They practice chewing people up and spitting them out for breakfast. It would be like the spider telling the fly to come into my parlor.

PREPARATION IS THE SAME REGARDLESS OF THE VARIOUS FALSE RELIGIONS

Know what you believe, Biblically, and be ready to give a sound Biblical answer (**1 Peter 3:15**).

It is not the author's intent to make the readers of this book experts on the Hebrew Israelites. Neither is it the author's claim or goal to be a scholar on the Hebrew Israelites. But many of the cults and false religions step on to our (Biblical) court, which is our Bible. It is here that we, Christians, should be spiritually bold, able to edify, and defend the faith as soon as they crack open our Christian book and proceed to quote from it (out of context).

- It is before we run into the cults and false teachers that Jesus instructs us to take His yoke upon us and learn of Him (**Matthew 11:29**).
- It is before the cults and false teachers snare our children and family members that we are instructed and warned to study (**2 Timothy 2:15**).

   1 Timothy 4:15-16 "Meditate upon these things; give thyself wholly to them; **that thy profiting may appear to all. Take heed unto thyself, and unto**

the doctrine; continue in them: **for in doing this thou shalt both save thyself, and them that hear thee.**"

James 5:20 "Let him know, that **he which converteth the sinner from the error of his way** shall save a soul from death, and shall hide a multitude of sins."

The question (or trap) is never how much do you know about the Hebrew Israelites, but rather how much do you know about what is in or not in your Bible?

- ☐ **Systematic Theology**[35] (what the whole Bible says about these particular subjects):
- ☐ **Theology Proper** (The study of the character of God)
- ☐ **Biblical Theology** (*study of the Bible, the Word of God*)
- ☐ **Christology** (The study of Christ (the man and his works))
- ☐ **Pneumatology** (The study of the Holy Spirit)
- ☐ **Soteriology** (*study of Salvation*)
- ☐ **Theological Anthropology** (The study of the nature of humanity)
- ☐ **Hamartiology (***study of Sin***)**
- ☐ **Angelology** (The study of angels)
- ☐ **Ecclesiology** (The study of the church)
- ☐ **Eschatology** (The study of the end time)

---

[35] Grudem, Wayne A. *Systematic Theology: An Introduction to Biblical Doctrine* (Making Sense of Series) (2009). Grand Rapids, MI: Zondervan.

Biblical Hermeneutics[36] is the study of the principles of interpretation concerning the books (text) of the Bible. Hermeneutics is both a science and an art. The purpose of Biblical hermeneutics is to help us to know how to properly interpret, understand, and apply the Bible. Applying Biblical hermeneutics protects us from misapplying Scripture or allowing bias to color our understanding of truth. God's Word is truth (John 17:17b).

- "The most important law of Biblical hermeneutics is that the Bible should be interpreted literally. We are to understand the Bible in its normal or plain meaning, unless the passage is obviously intended to be symbolic or if figures of speech are employed.

- A second crucial law of Biblical hermeneutics is that passages must be interpreted historically, grammatically, and contextually. Interpreting a passage historically means we must seek to understand the culture, background, and situation that prompted the text.

- A third law of Biblical hermeneutics is that Scripture is always the best interpreter of Scripture. For this reason, we always compare Scripture with Scripture when trying to determine the meaning of a passage."

First, the Bible is to be interpreted like any other book because it is a book originating with God, but utilizing fully the vocabulary, culture, background, and education of man. These things don't have the right to change scripture, but are valuable for giving you the background to understand scripture.

Second, to interpret Scripture, you need to understand that Biblical literature has prose or poetry, history, allegory,

---

[36] http://www.gotquestions.org/Biblical-hermeneutics.html Retrieved 6-4-2016)

literal, and symbolic language. We must understand which is which.

Third, one should have some sense of historical background so that we don't approach the Bible as though it were written now (today). But it must be approached in its historical context and the culture that produced it.

Fourth, we must understand geographical conditions, terrain, climate, and how people looked upon these things and what it meant to them. [37],[38]

Church History: Christ, Apostles, Early Church Fathers, Persecution, Constantine, etc.: THE CHURCH HISTORY presents a panorama of apostles, Church fathers, emperors, bishops, heroes, heretics, confessors, and martyrs.[39]

The Black Hebrew Israelites (BHI) study Biblical deception. Their approach and tactics are illogical and heretical. They practice **Eisegesis**[40], "the process of interpreting a text or portion of text in such a way that the process introduces their own presuppositions, agendas, or biases into and onto the text. In other words, they *read into* the text what is not there. This act is often used to "prove" a pre-held point of concern to the reader and to provide him or her with confirmation bias in accordance with his or her pre-held agenda."

According to one BHI camp website, Great MillStone (GMS) Homework: "All GMS members must cut like a sharp

---

[37] http://www.preteristarchive.com/Books/pdf/1883_terry_bib-hermeneutics.pdf (06-04-2016)

[38] Scripture Twisting: 20 Ways the Cults Misread the Bible Kindle Edition by James W. Sire (Author)

[39] Eusebius: The Church History Paperback – May 31, 2007 by Eusebius (Author), Paul L. Maier (Translator)

[40] https://en.wikipedia.org/wiki/Eisegesis Retrieved 06-04-2016

blade, so GMS have en-stated weekly tests which will be administered by your camp leaders."[41]

THE BLACK HEBREW ISRAELITES

The terms "Black Hebrews" and "Black Israelites" refer as a categorical whole to several independent sub-sects whose unifying characteristic is that their members are of black African descent who claim Hebrew/Israelite ancestry. Apart from this unifying characteristic, however, these sub-sects are very distinct from one another.[42]

There is nothing in the Bible to indicate or imply in context that Jesus or the apostles were black or white while He or they walked the earth. Glenn Usry and Craig Keener in their book, "Black Man's Religion," points out that Jesus was "probably, the same light-brown color as most other Jews who traveled a lot in the hot Mediterranean sun. After all, Jesus did not stand out in a crowd when he wasn't glowing (**John 7:10-11**). This is not to say that Jesus and his other Jewish contemporaries were Black Africans; it is merely to say that they were not White Europeans either."[43,44]

Jesus had physical characteristics (race) of and was religiously a Jew. A contrast would be the Ethiopian eunuch of **Acts 8:26-37**. It is clear from the text that he was by physical characteristics (birth) an Ethiopian who was a convert to the Jewish religion, who after receiving Jesus Christ became a Christian (follower of Jesus Christ), known as **the way (Acts 9:2; 19:9, 23; 24:14, 22)**. It would be a stretch of the imagination or eisegesis to imply that this

---

[41] https://www.youtube.com/user/GMShomework#p/a/u/1/LX5t6Lz1iXk Retrieved 06-04-2016

[42] http://www.gotquestions.org/black-hebrews-israelites.html Retrieved 05-13-2016

[43] Usry, Glenn; Keener Craig S. *Black Man's Religion: Can Christianity Be Afrocentric?* (Kindle Locations 861-864). Kindle Edition

[44] https://www.youtube.com/watch?v=rPT_uI2WoAw Retrieved 05/18/2016

eunuch man was either Hebrew, a Jew, an Israelite, or Spiritual Israel.

There were never prohibitions against Jewish-Gentile marriages as a racial mixture, but the prohibitions were strictly against believer-unbeliever marriages **(Deuteronomy 7:3-5)**

The Scripture tells us that Moses, **a Jew** by birth who practiced the Jewish religion as ordained by God, married **an Ethiopian** (Cushite) woman **(Numbers 12:1, KJV, NASB)**. No doubt because of her husband and the ordinances of God, she practiced the Jewish religion **(Leviticus 17:8,10, 11-15 34; Joshua 8:35)**. This Ethiopian woman is now an Israelite through marriage (customarily/ethically), and she is under the Jewish faith, but by birth she is still classed as an Ethiopian (physical characteristics).

The same would be with strangers (Ethiopians, Egyptians, etc.) who sojourned with the Israelites and many who eventually converted to the faith of the Hebrews (or Judaism). Many married within the culture, were fruitful, and their family multiplied. Even Jesus has gentile (regardless of race) ancestry through Rahab (Amorite) and Ruth (Moabite) (Matthew 1:5). But there is no ridiculous statement, as a fact, that all Amorites or all Moabites are Jews and/or they practice Judaism. In the same sense, history does not bear witness that Judaism was the black man's religion (in any form), or that the Jews or Hebrews were originally black. This is not a denial of the existence of historical Black Jews, or that there are no descendants today. What is being challenged are those who would have us rewrite the Bible or history in order that they might validate their need for identity, but at the cost of stealing another's identity, in this case the Jews.

According to Charles Whitaker in an article, "Proselytism Yesterday, Today, and Tomorrow (Part One)," "The Hebrew language lacks an exact equivalent to the Greek noun *proselyte*, which means a *newcomer* (*Strong's* #4339). However, in the Old Testament, God's law does allow the *ger* (*Strong's* #1616), usually rendered "stranger," to become a full-fledged citizen of Israel. To do this, he needed to become circumcised. **Exodus 12:48** addresses this changing of belief system in reference to the Passover.

The stranger "wants to keep the Passover." There is no hint of God expecting Israel to seek converts among the heathen by actively preaching to—or *at*—them. Here, there is no coercion, subtle or otherwise; the Gentile convert voluntarily gives himself to come under the Old Covenant. **Deuteronomy 4:5-7** states the dynamics of this conversion.[45]

> **Exodus 12:48-49** "And when a stranger shall sojourn with thee, and will keep the Passover to the Lord, let all his males be circumcised, and then let him come near and keep it; and he shall be as one that is born in the land: for no uncircumcised person shall eat thereof. One law shall be to him that is **homeborn**, and unto **the stranger** that sojourneth among you."

> **Deuteronomy 4:5-8** Behold, I have taught you statutes and judgments, even as the Lord my God commanded me, that ye should do so in the land whither ye go to possess it. Keep therefore and do them; for this is your wisdom and your understanding in the sight of the nations, which shall hear all these statutes, and say, Surely this great nation is a wise and understanding people. For what nation is there so great, who hath God so nigh unto them, as the Lord our God is in all things that we call upon him for? And what nation is there so great, that hath statutes and judgments so righteous as all this law, which I set before you this day?

---

[45] http://www.bibletools.org/index.cfm/fuseaction/Library.sr/CT/ARTB/k/1114/Proselytism-Yesterday-Today-Tomorrow-Part-One.htm

As soon as we start talking in terms of color (Black, White, yellow, mixed, etc.) in relationship to people we have left the Bible on the nightstand. God said, "Because It is written, Be ye holy, for I am holy" in **1 Peter 1:16**. God wants obedience and could care less about the race of a person:

> **Acts 17:26-27 And hath made of one blood all nations of men** for to dwell on all the face of the earth, and hath determined the times before appointed, and the bounds of their habitation; **That they should seek the Lord**, if haply they might feel after him, and find him, though he be not far from every one of us:

> **Galatians 3:28-29** There is neither **Jew nor Greek**, there is neither **bond nor free**, there is neither **male nor female**: for **ye are all one in Christ Jesus**. And if ye be Christ's, then are ye Abraham's seed, and heirs according to the promise.

> **Romans 2:28-29** For **he is not a Jew, which is one outwardly**; neither is that circumcision, which is outward in the flesh: **But he is a Jew, which is one inwardly**; and circumcision is that of the heart, in the spirit, and not in the letter; whose praise is not of men, but of God.

Even though God has already spoken, there have been literally hundreds of books written by people with Ph.D.'s following their name on the Black Man and his Lost Identity, and how they can help you discover who you are. While there are facts to be learned, skewed facts are no longer facts. Even so, people swear by these books as if they're historical and God co-authored them or wrote the raving reviews. It is my belief that we should use the same standard of testing instructed in the Scripture when reading those books:

> **1Thessalonians 5:21** "Prove all things; hold fast that which is good."

There are spin-offs from the Jews, Hebrews, Israel, Spiritual, Judah groups going in every direction contrary to Judaism, Christianity, or both. Some even include Egyptian mythological practices. There is no lack of seekers who eagerly join and follow these groups based on corrupt and/or false theology, and distorted historical facts.

According to Vocab Malone, a Christian minister and apologist at the Roosevelt Community Church in Phoenix, Arizona who manages streetapologist.com, the Hebrew Israelites don't prefer the title "Black Hebrew Israelite." They believe it is an inaccurate term or title because included in the Hebrew Israelites are other people of Mexican descent, Native Americans, etc. – the other eleven tribes. They would say we are not all black, but if you are black (not all) you are probably within the tribe Judah, the flagship that leads the movement. They prefer the term Hebrew Israelites, and believe they're the literal and physical descendants of Abraham. The awakened sons of Israel are now realizing their stolen heritage that was forgotten due to sin and God's punishment on Israel. But now the movement is being awakened to this reality. Their mission is not to convert people. They don't believe in conversion.

The Black Hebrew Israelite's mission is to:

1. gather the scattered - those other Black Hebrew Israelites that have not come into the knowledge of who they are.
2. proclaim judgment against the Edomite.

Based on the camp (similar to denominations) that one is in, there are some groups that believe there is no salvation for Esau's children (the so-called white man), and there are other groups that believe that anyone can be grafted into the nation, but it is through clinging to an Israelite.

Zechariah 8:23 "Thus saith the Lord of hosts; In those days it shall come to pass, that ten men shall take hold out of all languages of the nations, **even shall take hold of the skirt of him that is a Jew**, saying, We will go with you: for we have heard that God is with you."

All groups don't do street teaching. All groups don't use swearing and profanity in their teaching. Although still in error, some are kinder and gentler in their approach. Some camps mock the other camps calling them Christians, not that they are Christians. In fact, they deny many of the essentials of the Christian faith such as the Trinity, and the deity of Jesus Christ.

Vocab Malone's website http://streetapologist.com/ is an excellent resource on these groups and provides other apologetic information.[46]

Black Hebrew Israelites: also known as

- **Black Hebrews**
- **African Hebrew Israelites**
- **Hebrew Israelites**

They believe they are the **PHYSICAL** descendants of the ancient Israelites. Many of these groups were founded in the United States during the late 19th and early 20th centuries.

Their beliefs and practices vary considerably:

- Black Jews, who maintain a Christological perspective and adopt Jewish rituals.
- Black Hebrews, who are more traditional in their practice of Judaism.

---

[46] https://youtu.be/o2q9Q_7ZvHs Retrieved June 3, 2016

Other Groups: Hebrew ~ Israel ~ Jews

- Black Israelites, who are most nationalistic and furthest from traditional Judaism.

Black Hebrew Israelite Subgroups and Organizations:

- Commandment Keepers[47]
- The Law Keepers[48]
- African Hebrew Israelites of Jerusalem[49]
- Christian-affiliated
- Church of the Living God
- Church of God and Saints of Christ[50]
- Israelite Church of God in Jesus Christ[51]
- Israel United In Christ[52]
- Nation of Yahweh[53]
- GREAT Mill Stone (GMS)[54]
- Gathering of Christ Church[55]
- Israelite School of Universal Practical Knowledge[56]

---

[47] http://www.blackjews.org/Essays/DestructionofCommandmentKeepers.html Retrieved 09-18-2016

[48] http://www.thelawkeepers.org/ Retrieved 05-14-2016

[49] http://africanhebrewisraelitesofjerusalem.com/ Retrieved 05-14-2016

[50] http://cogasoc.org/wordpress/about/doctrine/ Retrieved 05-14-2016

[51] http://www.icgjcmd.org/ Retrieved 05-14-2016

[52] http://israelunite.org/ Retrieved 05-14-2016

[53] http://www.yahwehbenyahweh.com/ Retrieved 05-14-2016

[54] http://www.greatmillstone.info/ Retrieved 05-26-2016

[55] http://www.gatheringofchrist.org/ Retrieved 05-26-2016

[56] http://isupk.org/ Retrieved 05-26-2016

COMMANDMENT KEEPERS:

Founded by Wentworth Arthur Matthew in Harlem in 1919.

- Influenced by the non-black Jews, Marcus Garvey, and the Universal Negro Improvement Association.
- Learned about the Beta Israel (Ethiopian Jews) and identifies with them.
- Observes Jewish dietary laws and circumcision.
- Celebrates bar mitzvah.
- Separates (partitions) men from women in their synagogue during worship.
- Established the Ethiopian Hebrew Rabbinical College (later renamed the Israelite Rabbinical Academy).
- Believe they are descendants of King Solomon and the Queen of Sheba.

AFRICAN HEBREW ISRAELITES OF JERUSALEM:

Founded by Ben Ammi Ben-Israel in Chicago, Illinois, in 1966. In 1966 their spiritual leader, Ben Ammi, had a vision that it was time for the Children of Israel who remained in America (the land of their captivity) to return to the Holy Land (the land of their origin).

In 1967, after a claimed two thousand years in the Diaspora, four hundred Hebrew Israelites left America. According to their plan, they settled in Liberia's interior to purge themselves of the negative attributes they had acquired in the captivity. After spending a two-and-one-half year period in Liberia, The African Hebrew Israelites prepared to make the last portion of their journey home, a journey to Israel in 1969.[57]

- [ ] In about 1969. Ben Ammi and about 30 Hebrew Israelites **moved to Israel**.
- [ ] As of 2006, over 2,500 Hebrew Israelites live in Israel and are referred to as **Black Hebrews**.
- [ ] There are Hebrew Israelite communities in **several major American cities** including Chicago, St. Louis, and Washington, D.C.
- [ ] Believe they are descended of the Tribe of Judah who were exiled from Israel after the destruction of the Second Temple in 70 CE.
- [ ] Incorporate elements of African American culture into their interpretation of the Bible.
- [ ] Observe Shabbat and Biblically ordained Jewish holidays such as Yom Kippur and Passover.
- [ ] In accordance with their interpretation of the Bible, they follow a strictly **vegan diet** and wear only **natural fabrics**.
- [ ] Most men have **more than one wife**, and **birth control is not permitted**.
- [ ] Women follow the Biblical laws concerning menstruation, and newborn boys are circumcised.
- They **do not recognize rabbinical** Jewish interpretations such as the Talmud.

CHURCH OF GOD AND SAINTS OF CHRIST:

Founded by William Saunders Crowdy in 1896, in Lawrence, Kansas.

---

[57] http://www.religioustolerance.org/bhi.htm Retrieved 05-13-2016

The members of this congregation believe they are descendants of the lost tribes of Israel. In 1906, Prophet Crowdy passed his mantle of leadership to three successors: Chief Joseph W. Crowdy, Bishop William H. Plummer, and Counselor Calvin S. Skinner. Counselor Skinner consecrated for leadership Rabbi Howard Z. Plummer, who prior to his demise ordained Rabbi Levi S. Plummer. Currently, the congregation is led by Rabbi Jehu A. Crowdy, Jr. The Church of God and Saints of Christ has headquarters in Belleville (Suffolk), VA with tabernacles across the United States, Jamaica, and Africa.[58]

OT observances include:

- Circumcision of newborn boys.
- Use of the Hebrew calendar.
- Wearing of yarmulkes.
- Observance of **Saturday as the Sabbath** and the **Ten Commandments.**
- Celebration of Passover and other religious holy days.

NT observances include:

- Baptism (immersion).
- The consecration of bread and water as Christ's body and blood.
- Foot-washing.

Despite their name:

- They **adhere to Judaism** as their religion.

---

[58] http://www.religioustolerance.org/bhi.htm Retrieved 05-13-2016

- They **do not believe** in Christianity.
- They **do not believe** that Jesus was God nor the son of God.
- **Believe** Jesus was a strict adherent to Judaism and **a prophet sent by God**.
- **Believe** William Saunders was a prophet also.

Subscribe to:
- Belief in one God, **love for all mankind**.
- Belief that anyone, **regardless of race**, nationality, or ethnicity, can embrace Judaism and become a member.
- BELIEVE that the Ten Commandments are immutable.
- BELIEVE that there is a resurrection.
- BELIEVE that heaven and hell are not geographical locations.
- BELIEVE that Judaism is not a race but a religion. Hence, we prefer the term "Israelite" when referring to members of the Congregation.

ISRAELITE CHURCH OF GOD IN JESUS CHRIST [59]

The ICGJC and its various splinter groups can be loosely grouped together as sects which advocate a King James Version only approach to the Bible (i.e. they only endorse the KJV as Scripture):

- ☐ Believe that their supposed Israelite identity is based on the Bible, history, and archaeology.

---

[59] http://www.religioustolerance.org/bhi.htm

- Believe that white people are **Edomites** (it should be noted that other so-called "Black Israelite" sects declare white people to be descendants of **Japheth**), and claim to speak "Lashawan Qadash" (a form of Hebrew grammatically identical to Modern Israeli Hebrew, save for the absence of any vowel except 'a' and 'i').
- **The Black Israelites seen preaching on the streets** of many American cities are of this cohort.

* Unlike most BHI sects, **the ICGJC is also open to Hispanics and Native Americans, who are believed to be among the 12 tribes of Israel**. They produce a television program called "The Hidden Truth of the Bible," which airs on many public access stations across the country. Websites endorsing the views of this branch of the Black Israelite community include http://www.theholyconceptionunit.org.

NATION OF YAHWEH:

Founded by Yahweh Ben Yahweh (Hebrew for "God, son of God") in 1979, in Liberty City, (formerly known as Hulon Mitchell, Jr.) Florida. The group is also known as Nation of Israel, Tribe of Judah, Temple of Love, and etc.).

Teachings:

* God and all the prophets of the Bible were black.
* Blacks would gain the knowledge of their true history through him.
* Loyalty to himself, as the son of God YHWH.
* He was the living Messiah of the Nation of Yahweh.
* Whites and particularly Jews are infidels and oppressors.

Convictions: Conspiring to **murder white people** as an initiation rite to his cult, as well as **former members who disagreed with him**, in one case by decapitation.[60]

The Nation of Yahweh[61] is a predominantly African American group that is the most controversial offshoot of the Black Hebrew Israelites line of thought. It has often been labeled a hate group and was founded in 1979 in Miami by Hulon Mitchell Jr., who went by the name Yahweh Ben Yahweh. Its goal is to return African Americans, whom they see as the original Israelites, to Israel. The group departs from mainstream Christianity and Judaism by accepting Yahweh Ben Yahweh as the Son of God. In this way, its beliefs are unique and distinct from that of other known Black Hebrew Israelite groups.[62,63] The group has engendered controversy due to legal issues surrounding its founder and has also faced accusations of being a black supremacist cult by the Southern Poverty Law Center[64] and The Miami Herald.[65]

In 1979, Yahweh Ben Yahweh came to Miami and became the Spiritual Leader and Founder of The Nation of Yahweh. Although he took a vow of poverty, in seven years he guided The Nation to amass a $250,000,000 empire. Under his direction, The Nation of Yahweh has grown to encompass disciples, followers, and supporters in over 1,300 cities within the U.S. and 16 foreign countries. Yahweh is bringing about

---

[60] https://en.wikipedia.org/wiki/Yahweh_ben_Yahweh

[61] https://en.wikipedia.org/wiki/Nation_of_Yahweh (05-14-2016)

[62] *Gallagher, Eugene V. (2004). The New Religious Movements Experience in America. Greenwood Press.*

[63] Rebirth of A Nation." Southern Poverty Law Center. Retrieved 01-20-2008.

[64] Potok, Mark (Fall 2007). "Margins to the Mainstream." Southern Poverty Law Center. Retrieved 01-20-2008.

[65] Miami Herald article http://www.religioustolerance.org/bhi.htm Retrieved 05-13-2016

changes in the lives of individuals and is giving the world the keys to success in life Politically - Economically - Educationally - Socially - and Spiritually.[66]

RACISM AND ANTI-SEMITISM:

- They believe that the Tanakh forbids them from allowing "whites," —Jews of relatively light complexion whom they call "Caucasians" as opposed to Semites into their congregations.
- A number of Black Hebrew Israelite groups are thought of as racist.
- They insist that these "Caucasian," non-Semitic Jews, are not descended from Israelites at all, but rather from Edomites and Khazars. [67]
- Black Hebrew Israelite groups have been accused of anti-semitism; a term they reject since Black people are in fact Shemetic, choosing not to acknowledge the fact that, in modern usage and in this context, the term 'anti-Semite' almost exclusively refers to antagonism towards Jews.

CHURCH OF THE LIVING GOD:

Founded by F. S. Cherry, a Black Jewish movement called the Church of God, in Philadelphia in 1915. Theologically it mixed Judaism and Christianity, although the Jewish Bible and the Talmud were considered the essential Scriptures. Several Jewish practices and prohibitions were observed by Cherry's flock. The movement

---

[66] http://www.yahwehbenyahweh.com/ Retrieved 05-14-2016

[67] https://www.youtube.com/watch?v=kgb_WrYx2UA Retrieved 09-18-2016

has been reported to survive under the leadership of Cherry's son, but little information about it has been disseminated.[68]

THE HOUSE OF LEVI [69]

Universal Beliefs among the Hebrew Israelites:

- **Yah created** the heavens and the earth and everything in existence; **His flesh and Holy Spirit are one**. To his will all that exist shall submit.

- The trans-Atlantic slave trade was predicted in **Deuteronomy 28:68.**

- **The Torah is the sole superior authority** for all Israelites, all other scriptures are or can be beneficial and benevolent.

- The kingdom of Yah will be established and all of the saints of the Most High, who are **the Israelites, shall take the kingdom and possess it forever and ever.**

- All those who accept the Torah as the highest and unfailing law of Yah, and faithfully strive to obey it, is an Israelite.

- An Israelite who predicted something that comes to pass is a prophet of Yah.

COMMON BELIEF ABOUT THE TWELVE TRIBES OF ISRAEL

Many Hebrew Israelite groups believe and list the Twelve Tribes of Israel as follows:

---

[68] http://www.religioustolerance.org/bhi.htm Retrieved 05-13-2016

[69] http://haitianisraelites.weebly.com/25-beliefs-of-the-hebrew-israelites.html Retrieved 05-13-2016

1. **Judah** — Black Americans
2. **Benjamin** — West Indians
3. **Levi** — Haitians
4. **Simeon** — Dominicans
5. **Zebulun** — Guatemalans, Panamanians
6. **Ephraim** — Puerto Ricans
7. **Manasseh** — Cubans
8. **Gad** — Native American Indians
9. **Reuben** — Seminole Indians
10. **Asher** — Colombians, Uruguayans
11. **Naphtali** — Argentines, Chileans
12. **Issachar** — Mexicans

EXAMPLES OF BHI ON THE STREETS:

They can be very vulgar in their dialog with you even as they are quoting and reading scriptures when making their points on the streets.

Black Hebrew Israelites in Hollywood Blvd:
https://www.youtube.com/watch?v=XI1Zdt031r8

The Commandment Keepers Documentary:
https://www.youtube.com/watch?v=stKpJhTYn9I

A Young White Pastor gets his heart broken by the Hebrew Israelites:
https://www.youtube.com/watch?v=kgb_WrYx2UA

Who are the Hebrew Israelites:
https://www.youtube.com/watch?v=_Jck9MFWLTA

Who are the Hebrew Israelites 2:
https://www.youtube.com/watch?v=knOnkqXO9sI
Jesus Part 1
https://www.youtube.com/watch?v=0GeO1C3LQbY
Jesus Part 2
https://www.youtube.com/watch?v=oPCktqYwotg

All the above sites verified 09-18-2016

BHI DEFINITION OF GENTILES IN THE BIBLE

According to many Hebrew Israelites, **the word gentile** is not used in reference to non-Israelite nations in the Bible. It refers to non-believing Israelites or Israelites that had been disbursed among other nations.

- Hebrew Israelites teach that when Jesus gives the great commission to His apostles in **Matthew 28:19 "Go ye therefore, and teach all nations, ..."** He was sending them out to where the Jews had been scattered among the nations, using **James 1:1 "...to the twelve tribes which are scattered abroad, ..."**

- While they do acknowledge that gentile means a non-believer, they say it also means an Israelite who has been carried away into the philosophy of the world:

John 7:35 says, "Then said the Jews among themselves, Whither will he go, that we shall not find him? **will he go unto the dispersed among the Gentiles**, and teach the Gentiles?"

- They teach that Israelites had become Gentiles by serving other gods of Christianity, Islam, etc. Because of that, God had scattered them, Quoting from **Deuteronomy 28:64 "And the Lord shall**

scatter thee among all people, from the one end of the earth even unto the other; **and there thou shalt serve other gods, which neither thou nor thy fathers have known**, even wood and stone."

- ☐ They even teach that Cornelius was an Israelite, contrary to the text in **Acts 10:1-7**.

- • They contend that these Gentiles were Israelites who were exposed to the philosophy of the Greeks. They use **Ephesians 2:11** "Wherefore remember, **that ye being in time past Gentiles in the flesh, who are called Uncircumcision** by that which is called the Circumcision in the flesh made by hands."

- ☐ Hebrew Israelites believe that Jesus Christ is coming back to save only Israelites quoting

  Romans 9:4 "**Who are Israelites**; to whom **pertaineth the adoption, and the glory,** and **the covenants**, and **the giving of the law**, and **the service of God**, and **the promises**;

  Hebrews 8:8 "For finding fault with them, he saith, Behold, the days come, saith the Lord, when I will make a new covenant with **the house of Israel** and with **the house of Judah**:"

- • They don't believe that all nations shall be saved in Christ.

- • They quote the Apocrypha **2 Maccabee 6:6** "Neither was it lawful for a man to keep Sabbath days or ancient fasts, or to profess himself at all to be a Jew."

  - o They teach Israelites were not allowed to be called Jews and allowed themselves to be transformed into the Greek world and called themselves Greek. So the Israelites in Jerusalem were looking down on the Greek Israelites (Gentiles).

- Teaching that Christ died for the Israelites only, some explain GRACE like this: "Grace is what God is giving the Israelites. Time to get themselves together and **start keeping the law**. If they don't, when Jesus Christ returns He is going to kill them.

- BHI says the law was not done away with, but it was the punishment (works) that was done away with. In other words, we don't stone you. **Romans 3:31** "Do we then make void the law through faith? God forbid: yea, we establish the law.

- BHI explains the resurrection in **Romans 6:3-5** as getting rid of your old self (man) and becoming a new creature. The old man did things like eating pork (dietary laws) and committing adultery, etc.

- They refer to the works as **works of the law** meaning **the punishment of the law.**

BHI VS THE WHITE-MAN AND OTHER NATIONS

Black Hebrew Israelites (BHI) also known as Black Hebrews, or, Hebrew Israelites are groups of African-Americans situated mostly in the United States who **claim to be descendants of the ancient Israelites**. They are not to be confused with **African Hebrew Israelites** or **Beta Jews;** they claim that they are Alpha Israelites and that **they are not Africans** at all, but were merely sold into slavery from Africa.[70] Most BHI believe that the "white man" (Europeans) are descendants of Jacob's (Israel's) twin brother Esau (Edom) **(Genesis 25:25)**.

- They also believe that The Most High **has a stern punishment reserved for Esau's children,** at the end of days, for enslaving the Hebrew Israelites.

---

[70] http://www.religioustolerance.org/bhi.htm Retrieved 05-13-2016

- They believe **the White Man will be in heaven, but as slaves**. BHI teaches that according to **Isaiah 14:1-2** the white man is going to serve Israel as slaves in the kingdom of heaven.
- BHI teaches that the **"white man" (Europeans) are in their heaven now**, and they are the wicked that the earth has been given to in **Job 9:24**.
- According to many BHI teachers, Jesus only died and is coming back for the twelve tribes of Israel. All other nations will be punished; there is no salvation plan for them. BHI believes the Arabs (Ishmaelites), The Africans (Hamites) and the Europeans (Edomites) work together to enslave the House of Judah (Judah, Benjamin, Levi).
- Black Hebrew Israelites believe that the term Negros can be used to define the descendants of the **Trans-Atlantic Slave Trade slaves** and can be used to distinguish them from the **Africans (Hamites)**.
  - The BHI says that the real Jews are the Negros of America.
  - The Jews are one tribe of people - Judah.
  - They believe that you (the Negros) along with the other tribes are the real Israelites.
- BHI believes Jesus is black and all the prophets in the Bible are black.
  - **Black Hebrew Israelites practice separatism** instead of racism.
  - **BHI don't judge based on the color of one's skin**, but whether you are part of the Twelve Tribes of Israel or not
  - **BHI has no intention of uniting with the other nations under Jesus Christ**, because

they believe the Bible instructs them to separate from the other nations.

- BHI claim they are refugees of the so-called "**First Jewish-Roman War**" avoiding the holocaust at Masada In 73 AD. [71]
  - In 70 AD they claim to have fled Judea into the interior of West Africa, and they sojourned there some 1,500 years.
  - Their Shemetic ancestors were sold by Hametic Africans to Ishmaelite-Arabian slave traders, who, in turn, sold them to European Trans-Atlantic Slave Traders in the early 1600's.
- BHI uses and calls the Apocrypha inspired writings. They teach that God divided the nations and separated the sons of Adam from the children of Israel:

Deuteronomy 32:8 *"**When the most High divided to the nations** their inheritance, **when he separated the sons of Adam**, he set the bounds of the people according to the number of the children of Israel."*

They use 2 Esdras 6:54-56 to show that all came from Adam, but God only chose Israel, and the other nations he said were nothing to him but like spit:

2 Esdras 6:54-56 "And after these, **Adam also, whom thou madest lord of all thy creatures**: of him come we all, and the people also whom thou hast chosen. All this have I spoken before thee, O Lord, because thou madest the world for our sakes" "**As for the other people**, which also come of Adam, **thou hast said that they are nothing**, but be like unto spittle: and

---

[71] http://www.religioustolerance.org/bhi.htm Retrieved 05-13-2016

hast likened the abundance of them unto a drop that falleth from a vessel."

- BHI does not believe in heaven or hell in the Christian sense. For them heaven is **rulership**. They believe that right now that we're in the Caucasian heaven. Some call the Caucasians the devil or devils.

- The Black Hebrew Israelites **reject Islam**, the Qur'an, Khabbalah; BHI **refuses to be called Christian** or to be compared with Christians.

- BHI rejects the Talmud because it was written by Europeans during the first century.

THE IRRATIONAL MIND OF BLACK HEBREW ISRAELITES

Irrationality is cognition, thinking, talking, or acting without inclusion of rationality. It is more specifically described as an action or opinion given through inadequate use of reason, emotional distress, or cognitive deficiency. The term is used, usually pejoratively, to describe thinking and actions that are, or appear to be, less useful, or more illogical than other more rational alternatives.[72,73]

Illogical:

1. characterized by lack of logic, senseless, or unreasonable
2. disregarding logical principles

---

[72] Mead, Margaret. *Male and Female: The Classic Study of the Sexes* (1949, 1998) Quill: New York, NY. HarperCollins

[73] Fletcher, Joyce (March 1994). "Castrating the Female Advantage: Feminist Standpoint Research and Management Science." *Journal of Management Inquiry 3* (1): 74–82.

It is impossible to reason with a person who has a reprobated mind; God has given them over to that which is counterfeit. The Bible clearly tells us no man can come to Jesus Christ unless:

Who comes to Jesus?

- Those the Father **gives** (John 6:37)
- Those the Father **draws** (John 6:44-45)
- Those the Father enables.
- Those that have **heard** of the Father will come (John 6:45).
- Those that have **learned** of the Father will come (John 6:45).
- Those that are **given** (John 6:65)
- Those that **believe** (John 6:47, 69)

Scripture speaks of those who have not the love of the truth and of the delusion that God allows them to believe their own craftiness (lie) which comes to nothing. They are damned by their only lie which God allows them to chase because they received not (rejected) the love of the truth (**2 Thessalonians 2:10-12**). For both, the Hebrew Israelites and The Spiritual Israel Church & Its Army, the gospel of Jesus Christ (who He is and His works) is not enough for salvation. The salvation they seek is tied to the identity of their flesh (skin color) and good works (the law) and not to the faith that was once for all delivered to the saints (Jude 3-4).

Even so, we tactfully witness to them with the understanding that God has mercy on whom He will (**Romans 9:14–18**); If they are to be lost, let it be because they rejected the gospel, and not because we refuse to share the gospel (**Ezekiel 33:7-9**). It is best to divide and conquer; in other words, one on one. Black Hebrew Israel members like to be in numbers, talking loud, intimidating others while quoting or reading Scriptures (out of context) as if that provides authority to their error.

> **Luke 11:21-22** "When a strong man armed keepeth his palace, his goods are in peace: But when a stronger than he shall come upon him, **and overcome him, he taketh from him all his armour wherein he trusted, and divideth his spoils.**"

Don't fear them, God can make us aware of the enemy's tactics, if we have obeyed Biblical instructions to:

> "**Study** to shew thyself approved unto God, a workman that needeth not to be ashamed, **rightly dividing the word of truth.**" (**2 Timothy 2:15**)

> "Meditate upon these things; **give thyself wholly to them**; that thy profiting **may appear to all**." (**1 Timothy 4:15**)

> "Take heed unto thyself, and unto the doctrine; continue in them: for in doing this thou shalt both save thyself, and them that hear thee." (**1 Timothy 4:16**)

Don't allow yourself to be lead down the rabbit's trail (off track or subject). Stick to the Scripture at hand:

> "But shun profane and vain babblings: for they will increase unto more ungodliness." (**2 Timothy 2:16**)

> "But foolish and unlearned questions avoid, knowing that they do gender strifes." (**2 Timothy 2:23**)

> "...strive not about words to no profit, but to the subverting of the hearers." (**2 Timothy 2: 14b**)

We are to be "bold as a lion" (Proverbs 28:1), wise as serpents, and harmless as doves (**Matthew 10:16**).

Pray, ask, and be guided by the Holy Spirit;

Matthew 10:20 "For it is not ye that speak, but the Spirit of your Father which speaketh in you."

Be under the subjection of the Holy Spirit:

2 Timothy 2: **24-26** "And the Lord's servant **must not be quarrelsome** but kind to everyone, **able to teach**, patiently enduring evil, **correcting his opponents with gentleness**. God may perhaps grant them repentance leading to a knowledge of the truth, and **they may come to their senses and escape from the snare of the devil**, after being captured by him to do his will." (ESV)

Keep in mind the crowds and young youthful minds that act like sponges with knowledge as they gather round and about the BHI on the corners, empty lots, and college campuses. Many times your answers are for their benefit in hopes of keeping them from being snared by the Black Hebrew Israelites whose claim is to awaken the hearers to their true identity. We must be careful and wise with answers and statements of fact. It is better if we speak five words with understanding than ten thousand words and the audience has no clue what we're talking about (**1 Corinthians 14:19**). Our goal is never to show how much we know or edify ourselves, but to teach and lead others to Christ according to the will of God.

Always remember, if it had not been but for the grace of God, there go I.

GLOSSARY

ACUS - AT&T College & University Systems [Page 31]

Apologetics may be simply defined as the defense of the Christian faith. [page 85]

Biblical hermeneutics is the study of the principles and methods of interpreting the text of the Bible. [page 85]

Big Four - Detroit police used *Big 4* or *Tac Squads,* each made up of four police officers, to patrol Detroit neighborhoods, and such squads were used to combat soliciting. [page 35]

Christology is the study of Jesus Christ as He revealed in the Bible. Some of the issues studied are: His deity, His incarnation, His offices, His sacrifice, His resurrection, His teaching, His relation to God and man, and His return to earth. [page 85]

Eisegesis is when a person interprets and reads information into the text that is not there. [page 85]

Exegesis is when a person interprets a text based solely on what it says. That is, he extracts out of the text what is there as opposed to reading into it what is not there (Compare with Eisegesis). [page 85]

Hamartiology is the study of the doctrine of sin. [page 85]

Historical Revisionism identifies the re-interpretation of the historical record, of the orthodox views about a historical event, of the evidence of the event, and of the motivations and decisions of the participant people. The revision of the <u>historical record</u> is to reflect the contemporary discoveries of fact, evidence, and interpretation, which produce a revised history. [page 85]

Monogenes - The phrase "only begotten" translates the Greek word *monogenes*. This word is variously translated into English as "only," "one and only," and "only begotten." [page 96]

Nodding - A semi dreamlike state where an opiate user slips in and out of consciousness. [page 30]

Pornea - The Greek words "pornea" (often translated "fornication") and akatharsia (often translated "uncleanness") are key terms used to refer to sexual sins in the Christian Scriptures (New Testament). They appear dozens of times, particularly in the writings attributed to Paul, who concentrated a great deal on sexual sins. [page 118]

Replacement Theology is the teaching that the Christian church has replaced Israel regarding God's purpose and promises. [page 85]

Soteriology is the study of the doctrine of salvation.

Stress Unit - After the riot in Detroit Michigan, city officials created a special police task force called S.T.R.E.S.S. (Stop the Robberies, Enjoy Safe Streets). STRESS escalated the tensions between the police department and the city's residents. [page 35]

RESOURCES

WEB INTERNET LINKS VERIFIED LIVE:

http://freeingjohnsinclair.aadl.org/node/200055 (September 15, 2016) [page 40]

http://attic.areavoices.com/2011/11/ (September 15, 2016) [page 48]

http://id.loc.gov/authorities/names/n79021339.html (September 16, 2016) [page108 -Kapelud]

https://drive.google.com/drive/folders/0B5La9jT-2SAHZndCUU1QekZlWEk (September 17, 2016 -Spiritual Israel Church Shared Documents)

https://en.wikipedia.org/wiki/John_of_Patmos (September 17, 2016 [page 157])

https://drive.google.com/open?id=0B5La9jT-2SAHdnpKdW9WRUVZZGM (September 18, 2016 – Black Hebrew Israelites – shared documents)

http://bit.ly/2cmgrUH (September 18, 2016 – Black Hebrew Israelites – shared documents)

http://www.bibletools.org/index.cfm/fuseaction/Library.sr/CT/ARTB/k/1114/Proselytism-Yesterday-Today-Tomorrow-Part-One.htm (September 18, 2016 page 176)

http://www.blainerobison.com/bible/bible-abbreviations.htm Retrieved September 18, 2016

http://www.blackjews.org/Essays/DestructionofCommandmentKeepers.html Retrieved September 18, 2016

http://www.thelawkeepers.org/ Retrieved September 18, 2016

http://www.blackjews.org/ Retrieved September 18, 2016

http://africanhebrewisraelitesofjerusalem.com/ Retrieved September 18, 2016

https://www.youtube.com/user/vocabmalone/videos Retrieved September 18, 2016 http://www.isupk.org/ Retrieved September 18, 2016

http://www.gatheringofchrist.org/ Retrieved September 18, 2016

http://www.greatmillstone.info/ Retrieved September 18, 2016

http://www.yahwehbenyahweh.com/ Retrieved September 18, 2016

http://israelunite.org/ Retrieved September 18, 2016

http://www.icgjcmd.org/ Retrieved September 18, 2016

http://cogasoc.org/wordpress/about/doctrine/ Retrieved September 18, 2016

http://www.religioustolerance.org/bhi.htm Retrieved September 18, 2016

http://www.theholyconceptionunit.org/ Retrieved September 18, 2016

http://www.thecomforter.info/main/ Retrieved September 18, 2016

https://en.wikipedia.org/wiki/Nation_of_Yahweh Retrieved September 18, 2016

https://en.wikipedia.org/wiki/Yahweh_ben_Yahweh Retrieved September 18, 2016

http://haitianisraelites.weebly.com/25-beliefs-of-the-hebrew-israelites.html Retrieved September 18, 2016

https://www.youtube.com/watch?v=stKpJhTYn9I Retrieved September 18, 2016

https://www.youtube.com/watch?v=XI1Zdt031r8 Retrieved September 18, 2016

https://www.youtube.com/watch?v=kgb_WrYx2UA Retrieved September 18, 2016

https://www.youtube.com/watch?v=_Jck9MFWLTA Retrieved September 18, 2016 https://www.youtube.com/watch?v=knOnkqXO9sI Retrieved September 18, 2016

https://www.youtube.com/watch?v=0GeO1C3LQbY Retrieved September 18, 2016

https://www.youtube.com/watch?v=oPCktqYwotg Retrieved September 18, 2016

Bibles used (includes hardcopy and software copy):

The King James Version (KJV);
The New King James Version; (NKJV)
The English Standard Version (ESV);
The New American Standard Bible (NASB);
The International Version (NIV);
The Revised Standard Version (RSV);

ABOUT THE AUTHOR

By all appearances, Robert Anderson prospered under the doctrine of The Spiritual Israel Church & Its Army. In fact, in earlier years he trusted it as sound doctrine. A native of Detroit Michigan, Robert Anderson was a rebellious youth who ran away to the streets full of crime, drugs and death. After over 30 years of self-chosen agony he escaped the streets by joining what he now knows is a cult.

For 25 years, he embraced the organization's doctrine moving through the ranks of Deacon, Minister, Elder, and Assistant Pastor. A graduate of the organization's *Israel Spiritual School of Theology*, he was an Assistant Pastor at Temple #2 in Chicago, Illinois. Years later he became the Assistant Pastor of Temple #8 in Detroit, Michigan. It was within this Organization that he met his wife of over 30 years, Jo Ann.

Under the teaching and encouragement within the organization, Pastor Anderson received his GED, a degree from Wayne County Community College (WC3) in Associate of Applied Science Computer and Data Processing, a degree from Detroit College of Business in Bachelor of Business Administration; and with honors in both degrees.

A salaried employee of AT&T he learned about diversity, through the opportunity to work with people from various cultures and ethnic groups. As he traveled the USA for AT&T, he learned there was more to the world than the streets of Detroit. After several promotions and 30 years of service, Robert chose to retire and pursue his goals as an entrepreneur professional photographer and videographer.

Even so, by God's mercy through it all, at God's calling he walked away from the fallacy that he once zealously taught others. Pastor Anderson now dedicates his life to studying the sound doctrine of Scripture and apologetics with the hope of warning and teaching others how to come out and/or avoid the cults and false doctrine.

Today, as a Bible believing Christian he serves as an Associate Pastor licensed under Pastor Emery Moss Jr. at Strictly Biblical Bible Teaching Ministries. Over the years as he has attended various classes and recorded them for his own studies, Pastor Anderson was guided by the Holy Spirit to design a website www.bibletalkbbc.com where various class lectures (audios) and resource literature are available to those that have the desire to learn.

He and his wife, Jo Ann, witness together at Wendy's, McDonald's and anywhere else they can speak one-on-one and pass out tracts and cards pointing people to Jesus Christ.

You are invited to join Pastor Anderson for his weekly
Tele-Conference Bible Study on Tuesdays from
7:00 p.m. – 9:00 p.m.

Call in Number (248) 607-0611/Pin:14251

To contact Pastor Anderson

Email: truthseekersread@att.net
Website: http://www.truthseekersread.com

www.ingramcontent.com/pod-product-compliance
Lightning Source LLC
Chambersburg PA
CBHW070733020526
44118CB00035B/1274